1

The Landscape
Northern Sea
The Queen's Castle
Cottage of Our Mother in Green
Cottage of Our Mother in Black
Western Sea
Dark Forest
Una's Farm
Home Of Tessa's Mistress
Mercurial's Cottage
Eastern Sea
Sea of the Seven Holy Siblings
City of the Crepe Myrtle
Southern Sea
Road
Forest
Meadow
Water
Mountains

This book is magic.
It is marked with cunning knowledge.
The words within are twisted and miraculous.
The images represent figures and archetypes
Who never were and always have been.
Blessed by the Three Mothers and Seven Holy Siblings,
This book will offer protection and refuge to all those who
seek it, unless they be your enemy.
Within lies the guile of the Man in Black,
The endlessness of the Lady of Other,
And the prismatic spectrum of the Divine Androgyne.
This book is loving.
This book is cruel.
This book is full of life.
This book is full of death.
This book will charm.
This book will curse.
This book is marked with cunning knowledge.
This book is magic.

Cunning Words
a Grimoire of Tales and Magic

By Marshall WSL

Meet me at the crossroads
Where the man in black does stand
Meet me at the crossroads
Where he offers me his hand
Meet me at the crossroads
With the serpent and the crow
Meet me at the crossroads
To the other world we shall go

Cunning Words
a Grimoire of Tales and Magic

I. Cunning Tales: a Collection of Stories and Magic

II. Cunning Rhymes: Magic in Verse

III. Cunning Compendium: a Codex of Grimoires, Rites, and Extrapolated Charms, Spells, and Curses

Dedication

Without several people, this book could not have been made. First, I want to thank Olivia Graves for reading every story, draft, and poem I sent her. She inspired the Black Mothers namesake and a cunning reader might even find her very likeness is captured somewhere in this book. I'd like to thank Aaron Oberon and Roger J Horne for introducing me to the concept of folkloric witchcraft and especially Aaron for encouraging me to write my own tales to work magic with. I want to thank my podcast partner, Austin Fuller for being a confidant and wonderful supporter of my work. I want to send out a special thanks to Gemma Gary for opening me up to the world of traditional craft. With her books, Traditional Witchcraft: a Book of Cornish Ways, The Black Toad, and The Devil's Dozen, my practice took a new form changing my perspective forever.

I'm deeply grateful to my friend Jerett for helping me edit this book and to my best friend of 20 years, Kevin, for always supporting me and giving me the space to share my passion with him.

And finally, I'd like to thank the Spirits. They are always around whispering some of the thoughts and ideas you can read here in this very book.

Introduction

I was twelve when I discovered my first book of witchcraft. I remember seeing this big, glossy, blue book at the top of the shelf in a bookstore which was Raymond Buckland's Complete Book of Witchcraft. I saved up my lawn mower money for weeks to buy it and hide it under my bed. It was the start of a beautiful and ugly path into my craft.

As a young queer boy, I was already ostracized for being different even though I didn't know exactly how just yet. This lack of identity, this powerlessness led me to seek some form of empowerment. I had been obsessed with the icon and archetype of the Witch. The hat, the broom, the skirts, the capes, I loved it all. It spoke to me in a way that had me seeking any and all books, movies, and television shows that included witchcraft. Wicca was my gateway into this world. In the 90s, publications pushed the idea that witchcraft and Wicca were synonymous and it wasn't till many years later that I discovered it was not.

I had to unlearn many false histories to be honest with myself about what I believed in. I struggled. In my late twenties, I fell deep into the New Age, Law of Attraction, ascension/5D spiritualism movement and it only took a year or two to send me spiraling into toxic positivity, spiritual bypassing, and conspirituality. I knew something wasn't right. I had spent a good part of my early twenties completely dropping any form of religion or beliefs altogether and after escaping that New Age mindset, I set out to reclaim the joy witchcraft brought to me in my youth.

To my surprise, I discovered so much had changed in the last decade. People were sharing their books of shadows online. Thriving groups of practitioners had built online communities to educate, share, and debate occult theory/practice. When I was young, we had to special order the next book we wanted from the back of the book we were lucky enough to find. I live in Texas, a place also known as the Bible Belt and access to this information was so limited.

I began to find more information about different forms of craft, hermetic orders, closed practices, the differences in folk magic, practice vs. religion, etc., and most importantly, I discovered traditional witchcraft and animism.

Now it's important to understand, the term "traditional witchcraft" gets confusing because of the way each individual interprets the word "traditional". This description does not refer to some ancient line of craft that exist higher, better, or truer than any other. It only refers to a practice inspired by the cunning folk of past centuries, folklore, trial records, traditions (new and old,) and most importantly, the connection to one's land. Animism is the belief that spirit resides in all things. Your home, your car, your jewelry, your clothing, herbs, plants, trees, roots, and it goes even deeper. Sigils, ideas, and thought forms can take on their own spirit. When casting a spell and using herbs or sigils, those aren't just ingredients. They sure spirit allies.

I read books like Traditional Witchcraft and The Black Toad by Gemma Gary, The Crooked Path by Kelden, Besom Stang and Sword by Christopher Orapello and Tara-Love Maguire, Treading the Mill by Nigel G Pearson, a Deed Without a Name by Lee Morgan, Folk Witchcraft, and A Boom at Midnight by Roger J Horne. This built a new framework work of practice and as I explored working with these spirits, the threads of my craft began to weave a new tapestry of colors, textures, and weight. My idea of the binary dropped away and the queerness of witchcraft became all-encompassing. And when I say queerness, I don't just mean my own connection to my sexuality but my love and passion for the weird, the wild, and the in-between.

I made connections with spirits, archetypal and literal. I began to write my own spells and built a court of sacred

and profane beings. My exploration into Chaos magic with
Liber Null by Peter Carol and Condensed Chaos by Phil
Hine taught me about creating magical sigils, world
building, and thought forms. These created thought forms
were birthed from my mind and I felt I had no choice but
to write them down.

Art would inspire me to the point of desperately needing
to know more about the characters I'd see in a sketch or
painting. What was their back story? Why are they smiling
or crying? Who is that in the background? What secrets do
these images know? What have they seen throughout
history? I blame the spirits and my curious imagination.

In January of 2022, I began with a challenge online: share a
piece of occult art that inspires you and write a short story
from the image in the caption. I chose an image from artist
Marco Megrati of a witch being burned at the stake but
instead of being fearful, she was leaning forward to light a
joint on the flames. This was that story.

*In 1607, my family turned me into the local inquisitors as a Witch.
They dunked me in the local river over and over till I almost
drowned. After days of torture and sleeplessness, I finally confessed to
signing my name in the Dark Lord's book hoping that would mean
salvation. Instead, I was sentenced to burn. As the heat began to rise
at my feet, I saw my family in the sea of faces watching, the children*

roasting meat and corn at the edge of the flames. Spoils of the bounty on my head. They thought they were finally free of me. They had no idea their betrayal had sealed their fate. As the fire grew, I leaned forward to light my flying joint, and just as I was feeling slightly more than toasted, I smirked at the crowd and flew away laughing at their fading horrified gasps. Over the last 5 centuries, I've changed identities more than 57 times running from my family's descendants, defying death due to my deal with the Old One. But I refuse to hide any longer. That's why I've finally decided to hunt them down one by one. There can be no other Southern Lights left... than me.

I continued to create stories that came to me as I write them. Old medieval woodcuts became prints of ideas about witches and I felt called to write the tale hidden within the lines. Planets and Days became personified. Folk names for cunning folk like Old Mother Red Cap, Green Cap, and Black Cap spiraled into figures with tales of magic, blessing, and bane. They took on a life of their own and have been transcribed in these pages.

In this book, you will read stories you've never heard before. You'll read about witches, devils, bargains, spirits, love, loss, heartbreak, death, life, and rebirth. There are tales that teach magic and spell craft, poems that share recipes, and narratives to inspire your practice. At the back, you'll find a collection of rites extracted from these stories, and lessons that will aid you in building your own framework of magic.

I want to be very clear. This book is a direct reflection of what has inspired my craft and my own personal gnosis. I do not claim to be of any ancient lineage, or that the tales and magic in this book are from some secret mystical origin. They are written by me from a place of creative epiphanies inspired by the old craft of those who came before me. Be sure to read this book in the arrangement in which it's been written as you are meant to receive information in a specific order. DO NOT attempt to work the magic in this book without fully reading and analyzing the stories and poems first. You will not yet know the energies you are calling upon or have the credence to properly work these rites.

I've been told that if I want to find the best book of witchcraft for me, I'd have to write it myself. This is that book. It's written for the most cunning, so pay close attention, and the spirits within just might inspire you to write your own story.

Marshall the Witch of Southern Light

The 1st of many author's notes: You'll find throughout this book author's notes just like this one. Pay special attention to these as they will inform you more deeply about the content within.

You'll also find a full space between paragraphs because I personally struggle with keeping attention when I'm overwhelmed with walls of text. It is my sincerest hope that this will help other neurodivergent readers who experience this and aid in more smooth and comfortable reading comprehension.

This book contains blood magic. This will involve using safe and sterile methods of pricking a finger for certain workings. You'll also see some animal parts are used. If this does not suit your practice, I suggest avoiding those rites or finding ways to adapt them to your practice.

Lastly, the herbs, spells, and remedies in this book are not to be used instead of a medical professional. Always speak with your doctor about adding new supplements and ingestible plants to your lifestyle. Never consume poisonous materials and wash your hands after working with the tools within this book.

Preface

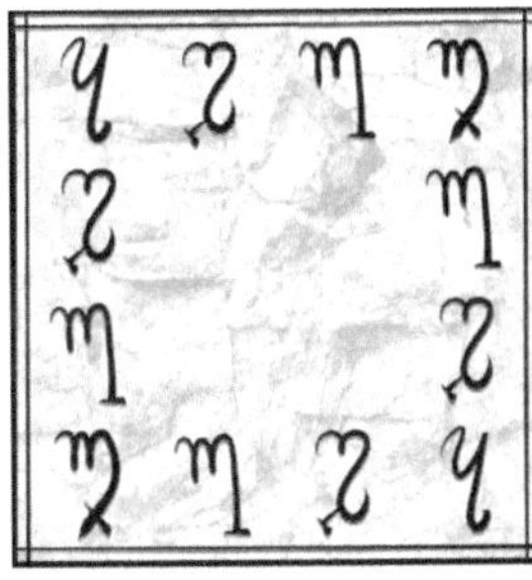

In the beginning, there was Absence and with the first spatial inversion, Existence entered this universe. Absence and Existence clashed, and from their irruption, Desire was born. As Absence and Existence intertwined and expanded, the desire for more lit the darkness with the stars. As Existence coalesced, attracted to the star's light by Desire, worlds spiraled into reality. Existence split into new forms and Desire gave birth to Physicality. Worlds spun and danced through the Absence singing to life. On one particular world, Physicality took strange new forms. Desire and Physicality made life and with that, cells began to form. Cells became complex organisms, and those organisms became the flora and fauna of this world. As Desire pressed on and Physicality pushed through the Absence, consciousness expanded and the fauna evolved. A spark of intelligence burst from Existence and the first primate stood. Desire turned survival into curiosity, and with curiosity, art was born. Following art came language, and after language came community. Absence, Existence, Desire, and Physicality saw what they created and for the first time, intelligent beings saw the Old Ones…

And this, dear readers, is where our stories begin.

I. Cunning Tales:

a Collection of Stories and Magic

1. Spirit Contracts

The Man at the Crossroads waited, their black hat shading their face, and a robe of darkness hid them in the night. They waited there as guardian and gatekeeper, ready and willing for one so cunning and brave.

One night, at the stroke of midnight, on the eve of the full moon, a woman approached the easternmost way. She stopped and pulled down her hood while the Man in Black waited in the shadows and watched. She lit a candle and began to walk counterclockwise from east to north, north to west, west to south, and back to the east again circling the crossroads. Three times did she go round all while chanting:

Man in Black,
Lord of the Crossroads,
I conjure you here!
I conjure you here!
I conjure you here!

The Man appeared before the woman and said, "Lady of the night, why do you come to the crossroads?"

"I come to make a trade," she replied. "I offer you dark bread from my home for a boon."

"What an offering," exclaimed the Man in Black, and they ate it up hungrily. "Come back again at the same time tomorrow and bring with you red wine to compliment the bread." She turned and left, and returned the following night.

Under the full moon, she encircled the crossroads again three times starting in the east while chanting:

Man in Black,
Lord of the Crossroads,
I conjure you here!
I conjure you here!
I conjure you here!

The Man appeared before the woman and said, "Lady of the night, why do you come to the crossroads?"

"I come to make a trade," she replied. "I offer you red wine from my home for a boon".

"What an offering," the Man in Black exclaimed and drank it in a single gulp. "Come back again at the same time tomorrow and bring with you a red thorny rose to compliment the bread and wine." She turned and left, and returned the following night.

Under the light of the moon's day-old fullness, she encircled the crossroads again three times starting in the east while chanting:

Man in Black,
Lord of the Crossroads,
I conjure you here!
I conjure you here!
I conjure you here!

The Man appeared before the woman and said, "Lady of the night, why do you come to the crossroads?"

"I come to make a trade," she replied. "I offer you a red thorny rose from my garden for a boon."

"What an offering," exclaimed the Man in Black as she handed them the rose. They took both their hands and placed them around her fist holding the stem and squeezed. Blood wept from between her fingers as the thorns bit into her palm yet she neither flinched nor made a sound.

"You offer me food and drink, beauty and blood. I accept your offerings and have gifts to bestow. Tell me, what is it you ask of me and I shall deliver it to you," said the Man in Black.

She looked deep into the darkness shaded by the wide-brimmed hat and told them her deepest desire.

And deliver it they did…

Author's note: This parable tells a story with no beginning and no end. It tells a tale of initiation and the bones of one of many kinds of spirit contracts. The Man in Black has been spoken of in folklore and trial records and depicted in early mid-millennium woodcut prints. They have been known as an initiator to witches coming out of dark forests or the shadows of the crossroads. They are a spirit of liminality and a physical gatekeeper to magic and the nonphysical. Consider this story an inspiration for your own spirit initiation.

2. The Hidden Book

There once was a young woman named Una who lived in a house outside of her western seaside village at the edge of an ancient forest. There she lived her days peacefully under a great oak, tending to her small farm, and taking care of her grandmother and her little pet bird.

Growing up, her granny had always read her stories of old gods that created our world, magic, fairytales, and of the creatures who lived in the forest behind their house. She told her how they once freely roamed this land and would one day take it back. She showed her how to leave out bowls of milk and whiskey at the trunk of the old oak to appease them. Una always thought these were peculiar old tales but when her granny got a bad back, she continued the task for her.

The townspeople had always thought they were a queer bunch ever since an incident with Una's mother before she was born. They lived too close to the wild and still dallied with blasphemous talk of the fair folk. Even the town mute who lost his will to speak for as long as Una could remember was weary of her and her Grandmother.

One day, a plague swept through the village leaving death and despair in its wake. The townsfolk in fear for their lives began to whisper of a witch's curse.

"This sickness ain't natural."

"It can only be the work of the devil."

"It must be the old fairy woman at the edge of the forest!"

"She's evil just like her daughter was!"

The fear and hysteria spread, working the villagers into a frenzy. They took up torches and pitchforks and, as a mob, marched to the little house at the edge of town.

"Send out the old witch!"

"We know you're in there, woman!"

"Give us the devil's whore or we'll burn your house down!"

Una was frightened but her granny held her hand and with resignation, "It will be all right, my darling. Go to my room, lock the door, and fear not. This house holds a strong power in its foundation." She did as she was told, locked the door, and hid under her grandmother's bed.

Moments later, she heard the sounds of the front door unlatching, and her grandmother say, "I've been waiting for you and after all these years, you've finally come. Leave my granddaughter be and I will come willingly." Terrified, Una covered the scream threatening to escape her mouth and cried silently.

When the voices had gone and the commotion had subsided, she crawled out from under the bed and unlocked the bedroom door. She made her way to the front, peered outside, and let out a blood-curdling wail. There she saw the lifeless body of her beloved granny hanging from the large oak.

It stormed as Una wept, and she couldn't tell the tears from the rain. She cut down the branch that held her grandmother and dug a grave below. Her grandmother's pet bird watched from the branches above. She laid her to rest within the roots of the tree, said goodbye, and made her way back inside.

Exhausted and feeling lost at what to do next, she made her way to the hearth to stoke the fire when a stone at the bottom corner of the mantle came loose. Behind it, she found the old book of stories. Una's Granny had insisted she learned to read, telling her one day it would be very important. She pulled the book out, opened the cover, and read the first brown-stained page.

Fair folk of the wood
I offer spirits and milk
Keep me kindly in your eye
For I give reverence To your ilk

For this trade
grant me your favor
Magic reveal
By blood on paper

She flipped through the pages but they were all blank, and just when she was beginning to question her memory, one of the corners of the pages sliced the tip of her finger. Drops of crimson soaked into the paper, bright red next to the old brown stains.

The fire shot up frightening Una, and shadows cast out all directions. She remembered the stories her Gran had read to her, stories of magic and making deals. She looked down at the blood-stained page and began to flip through the book curiously. Fading into existence we're beautifully written words. Not just words but stories, charms and spells, brews and powders, glyphs and instructions.

She spent hours reading the magic within the old leather tome memorizing words to make fire and rain, healing herbs to make bleeding stop and fevers break. There were powders with egg shells and cow dung to coax up from the ground a good harvest. She read of potions with mugwort and lemon grass that bring prophetic dreams, and instructions to divine with bones.

All these years her Granny's secret had kept them healthy and prosperous. If only she was still here to teach her now. Just then, the book in her lap leaped open. The pages turned of their own accord and there it was, "To call a Lost Ancestor" it said in swirling letters:

Into fire cast:
-the foot of a crow
-a twig of yew
-dried wormwood

-an item of the loved one you wish to speak with
-blood from the pointer finger of your left hand.

Gaze into the fire and chant:

Blood calls to blood
(Spirit's name) I conjure thee
A vision in flame
Come forth and here be

She spent the next few days collecting the necessary items and gathering her courage to speak with the dead. She waited till nightfall and was so nervous she barely touched her dinner. She sat in front of the fire, tossed in the crow's foot, the yew twig, the wormwood, and her gran's old nightcap, and pricked the finger of her left hand to flick a few scarlet drops into the sizzling fire. Then she said the words:

Blood calls to blood
Grandmother I conjure thee
A vision in flame
Come forth and here be

Sparks flew and for a moment she saw in the flames a glimpse of her granny's knowing smile. She said it again and eyes started to take shape. She said it again. "Don't be frightened, my darling," she heard her granny's voice, but the sound came through the hissing and crackling of the cinders. She said the words one final time and she saw before her in the fire her beloved grandmother.

Una cried out, "Oh granny why didn't you tell me?"

"Long ago, when your mother passed, I promised to keep you safe. I prepared you as best I could, my child. Magic can be a dangerous thing to play with, especially around narrow minds."

The grandmother continued, "I have grave news for you, my grandchild. My death will not stop the sickness ravaging the village. One day soon they will come for you too and you must prepare."

Una steeled herself to listen to her grandmother's instructions.

"With the branch of oak you cut my body from, whittle a staff and coat it with the ash from this fire and blood of your right hand. Just a drop will do! In the book, you'll find a sacred circle with the names of the ancient Old ones etched within. With the staff, draw it in the ground underneath the oak tree. When they come, they will not be able to cross. Tell them to leave and never return or they will meet an end far worse than any plague or sickness. If they do not leave peacefully, say the words:

Spirits of the wood
Fair folk hear my plea
I offer you blood of the guilty
Feast, drink and be free

Do not leave the circle till it is safe. Can you do this, child?"

"I think so," Una responded.

Her gran continued "Now, next you must collect three leg bones of a chicken and boil them till clean of flesh. Hold them in your crossed palms, anoint them with oil of Artemisia and your saliva then say:

Bones of my land
Only truth do tell me
If ye fall vertical
A yes my answer be

If the answer be no
On the horizon do fall
Spirits of my land
Your knowledge I do call

Toss the bones each morning to know if it is the day the villagers come. And my darling, be brave. It will be bloody, and your life will never be the same, but you will survive." She smiled with sadness in her hot coal eyes and with the crack of a burning log, and a hiss of sparks, she was gone.

Una had no time to think. She set to boiling the chicken leg bones in the hearth kettle and carving down the old oak branch as instructed. By dawn, the staff was complete and she coated it with ash from the hearth and blood of her right hand. She then cast the bones before her. When they landed on an even horizontal plane, she knew it was safe to rest. With great effort, she made her way to her bed and collapsed into a deep dreamless sleep.

A day and night later, she awoke hoping it had all been a dream, but upon seeing her blackened and cut-up hands, she knew. She cast the bones to find she had another day safe and continued to do so for the next three days. Each morning the bones were cast and each time at least two fell, ends pointing side to side. But on the third day, all three lay vertically. Today, they would come.

Outside she went with the staff, her bones, the book, and the face of courage and defiance. She drew the sacred circle around her under the tree. The wind blew the leaves

and the wildflowers swayed, but not a single blade of grass
moved within the lines of her circle. There she waited…
but not for long.

Soon the light of torches and sharp tips of pitchforks made
their way up the hill toward the house. They stopped
slightly unsure when they came upon Una with her staff in
her circle. "Una?" One of them ventured to ask, "is that
you?" Una did indeed look different, wilder, with an air of
otherness. Her hair and skirts were still and unmoving in
the wind as if standing in an entirely different world.

"WITCH!" One of the villagers screamed! "DEMON!"
shouted another. Forward they marched til they were a
stone's throw away from the tree and Una.

With voices that shouted and whispered, voices more than
her own, she commanded, "Leave this land and never
return or you will meet an end far worse than any plague
or sickness!" The town's people cowered in fear at the
inhuman voices coming from her. Una, the sweet young
woman now wild and ethereal. Some even started backing
away, terror flooding their eyes. But the voice of a man in
front rang out, "We rebuke your power, Witch! If you will
not hang, you will burn!" And with his vibrato, they
advanced.

She knew it was now or
never and said the
words her grandmother
taught her:

Spirits of the wood
Fair folk hear my plea
I offer you blood of the guilty
Feast, drink and be free

The words came out like
ribbons of magic
swirling in the wind, echoing amongst the trees. The
villagers froze. Terrified, they become silent as the echoing
whispers grew louder. The ground began to shake as roots
shot up from the earth impaling several men in the mob.
Blood sprayed and the townsfolk screamed.

A cloud of winged
creatures burst from the
forest led by her Gran's
pet bird. Beasts with
sharp teeth and glowing
red and gold eyes.
Rabbits that weren't
rabbits, pigs that weren't
pigs. Spirits flew through
the sky leading an army
of fairies, monsters, and
otherworldly beings.
They tore through the
flesh of the fleeing

villagers following them all the way into the city center. Buildings went up in flames and the smoke rose up in a cloud of crimson screams.

Una watched from her hill under the oak tree safe in her circle. She watched as the villagers who killed her Granny burned. She watched as the ground soaked up their blood swallowing their hate and hypocrisy. *I guess Granny was right* she thought as she remembered the fairy stories she had told her. The stories of the hidden ones of the wood who would one day reclaim their land.

And for that night, they did.

She watched the carnage with a crooked smile as a glistening tear fell from her eye. Her Gran's pet bird landed on her shoulder. He looked at her, at the bloody scene below, and sighed as if to say, "Isn't it just beautiful…"

3. First Flight

Meet me at the crossroads
Where the man in black does stand
Meet me at the crossroads
Where he offers me his hand
Meet me at the crossroads
With the serpent and the crow
Meet me at the crossroads
To the other world we shall go

He applied the greasy ointment to his forehead, behind his ears and neck, to his chest and armpits, then let his palms slide down to his groin where it slid between folds of swelling flesh. He continued to glide the slick substance to his feet and even between his toes.

He sat there naked and unafraid at the hearth as the dying embers still heated his oily skin. He breathed deeply, chanting the words. In four counts and out four counts, in five counts and out five counts, in six counts and out six counts, and his heart rate slowed. The edges of his vision began to blur and he slowly lowered himself totally to the floor.

He chanted and breathed till his spirit slick with the grease slipped out of his skin and stood. He took the staff propped up against the mantle, placed it between his thighs, and allowed the soles of his feet to rise off the ground. His toes lifted and he floated there for a moment completely weightless, lighter than a feather.

It was his spirit that was flying, not the staff as it was predominantly to aid in steering as wind currents were slightly difficult to navigate some nights. He pointed the tip of the staff at the chimney opening and willed himself forward.

Outside his window, the eyes watching him widened. She had known something had shifted in her neighbor and long-time friend. She had seen his appearance and confidence change ever so subtly over the past few months. She had seen the light coming out of his window

late at night and couldn't help but sneak out of her cottage
to get a peek.

In her wildest dreams, she never would have expected to
see him naked let alone flying. She watched as the twin tips
at the bottom of the forked staff disappeared up the
chimney and gasped. She stood back and peered up into
the night. The full moon lit up the sky and she saw as his
sleek body seemed to float amongst the stars and he soared
away.

This was her chance.

She slipped in through the unlatched window and made
her way to the chimney. There on the mantle was a small
clay jar of ointment and a scroll rolled up next to it.

She opened the lid and gave it a sniff. It had an herbal
aroma and was a slight, yellowish-green color. She began to
disrobe and rubbed it on her forehead, temples, neck, and
armpits. She then continued to her breasts and veered
downward to her groin. There she touched herself with a
quickening of breath. It made her feel lightheaded with a
heightened sense of awareness. She moved down her legs,
to her feet and toes, then stood there for a moment and
thought, "*what next?*"

She saw the scroll and unrolled it to see the small slanted
words scratched into the parchment in red.

Meet me at the crossroads
Where the man in black does stand
Meet me at the crossroads

She began to say the words and felt something within her jump. It was strange. She didn't jump but something within her did. She sat down next to her neighbor's body and said the words again, trying to relax. She lay down on the floorboards and continued to chant. Slowly her spirit began to slip out of her skin. The grease easing her soul's exit from her body.

She felt the whispering of the wind rush down the chimney. She said it again and could feel her center of gravity begin to lift. She said it again and felt her toes raise from the ground. Naked, she floated just feet off the floorboards and started to grab out at the air. "How did he do this?" she said aloud.

That's when she saw the old broom in the corner of the kitchen area. "Of course!" she exclaimed as she remembered the staff. Without some sort of rudder, she'd just continue sailing through empty air. She twisted her body and leaned towards the corner where the old broom lay lazily.

She grabbed the handle and swung it in between her legs. She wrapped one ankle around it and used her other leg to push off the wall as she turned the tip towards the chimney opening. She slowly glided toward the mantle, and as soon

as she had the broom tip up the flue, she said the words
one final time:

> *Meet me at the crossroads*
> *Where the man in black does stand*
> *Meet me at the crossroads*
> *Where he offers me his hand*
> *Meet me at the crossroads*
> *With the serpent and the crow*
> *Meet me at the crossroads*
> *To the other world we shall go*

As the words passed through her lips they echoed out like ribbons of whispers propelling her off the ground while simultaneously pulling her skyward.

 She saw the chimney opening come closer and closer, and the starry night sky exploded around her as she shot into the air. She held her eyes shut tight and clasped onto the broom for dear life but then she opened them and gasped as she took in the view.

She was high in the sky, the wind swirling in her hair and against her skin. The feeling of weightlessness and the freedom she had never felt locked to the ground was breathtaking. She had not a care in the world as she soared towards the mountains beyond the village, the castle, and the forest's edge.

As she got closer to the mountain top, she began to see other night flyers in the sky. One was on horseback and another atop a goat. Several were strode upon brooms like her and others had their knees tightly wrapped around a sleek wooden staff with two and sometimes three forks on one end.

They were all naked or clothed in sheer gossamer fabrics that flowed like liquid poured in the wind. She realized they were all descending atop the mountain peak to gather around a grandiose old tree. She slowly drifted down as well and upon touching down ever so softly, she realized she couldn't see anyone's face. Their legs, their arms, their hair, and bodies she could see, but every time she tried to make out a face, it seemed to blur.

She looked around to take in the dark scene around her. She was standing in the center of an old dirt road leading directly to the old tree. She saw as she began to circle its base three more roads at each quarter creating a sort of compass going in each direction.

As she circled, the others began to follow. At first, she thought she'd been found out, till she heard not shouts or pointed fingers but laughter. A violin struck up a few cords and there was a sound of drums that seemed to come from the tree itself. They were dancing.

She followed the group in a circle skipping widdershins around the tree and the music became louder. She closed her eyes and began to lose herself in the music. She laughed with the others as she danced. She had been told about the wickedness of dancing, but how could something that feels this joyous be wicked?

With each step, she felt lighter and lighter till her next step never came. With the broom in hand, she began to float alongside several other faceless bodies. She swirled in the air, hair floating all around her. Heat built in her center but the night air cool on her skin.

She saw as she danced in the air, the Man in Black stepping out from behind the tree, violin in hand. They were playing so beautifully, so furiously that the strings began to smoke. She couldn't see their face as it was nothing but an empty void of blackness. Their wide-brimmed hat and robes were black as pitch.

She was drawn down to the ground again so magnetic was their pull. She stared into the blackness under the brim of the hat and could almost make out a face but not quite. Was it soft and feminine? Was it angular and masculine? Was it both or neither? She couldn't tell and came closer still.

"Who are you?"

With no lips to speak, she heard them in her mind. "We are one and we are all. We are the physical Gatekeeper of the Old Ones. We are the shadow in the darkness and the flame that creates it. We are the line between pleasure and pain; sickness and health; heaven and hell. We are the being of the crossroads, the shade of midnight and midday, the dawn of sunrise, and the dusk of sunset. We are you and not you. Take our hand and let us show you what we have to offer." The Man in Black held out their hand; she closed her eyes and took it.

The figures dancing in the air around the tree began to drift toward her and she felt excitement override any fear. Hands came from all directions and began to caress her skin and the blur she once saw obscuring their faces faded away. As a virgin, she had always known one day she would be forced to give her body to the husband her family had chosen, but this was different. This was her choice. The heat in her center grew and her excitement rose as she softly moaned, "yesss."

She felt lips touch her shoulders, then calves, followed by the small of her back. Gliding through the air they sailed around her touching and caressing. Soft moans became louder as she felt a mouth below and a tongue encircle her swelling flesh. Lips met her ears, her toes and she threw her head back in pleasure she'd never felt before.

She heard a man's voice, one so familiar, whisper into her ear, "I knew if you watched, you would follow." She opened her eyes to see her neighbor. He continued, "I couldn't just tell you. No one can convince another to choose this path. It must be yours to decide." She wrapped one arm around his back and a thigh around his hips. She felt him below, and with her leg she pulled him in closer. He slowly entered her, causing her to gasp aloud with a shocking pain that turned to pleasure from all the hands and lips grazing her body.

The experience was real and unreal, a dream but she was wide awake. They were there, but nowhere. She felt herself shift and change as the wind blew around them and she felt him leave her body and she in turn grew hard and entered his. His eyes widened and the sound of shock and rapture escaped his throat. She thrust into him over and over giving no attention to the illogical nature of it. She knew it was an unnatural act, a perversion of her role as a woman… and she reveled in it.

She closed her eyes with the pressure building and opened them to see a black facelessness, wide-brimmed hat, and robes. She blinked and the man was again her neighbor. She closed them again and could feel the hat atop her head and black lighter-than-air robes flowing from her own body. She opened her eyes to look down and see her own legs and arms once more.

The pleasure built and she knew. She was they, and they all were her. She felt everything everywhere from everyone all at the same time and an explosion burst outward as they all moaned in pulses of electric satisfaction and initiation.

It was then that she knew the line between pleasure and pain. It was then she understood the crossroads between life and death, heaven and hell, light and dark. She had become one with the Man in Black, the spirit of magic, the Mage of In Between. The gates were open to the want of Desire, the spark of Existence, and the void of Absence. Her eyes saw now with crystal clarity as she opened them and let go of the hand the Man in Black offered her. She was still standing in front of the figure. Had that really happened? Was that all in her mind?

The breathless naked gathering all slowed their sinistral airborne dance and looked over the horizon as it began to lighten. Their voices rang out in unison, "Here we meet and here we shall part. Until we meet again." She felt one with them now, knowing the words, she spoke them as well.

The others began to saddle up their horses, goats, brooms, and staffs and lift off into the air down the mountain. She saw her neighbor who gave her a smile and beckoned her to follow. They lifted off and flew down the mountainside into the underbrush of the forest till they spotted the chimney they had both flown out of at the midnight hour.

They glided down till their feet met the ash of the hearth. They saw their bodies laying naked on the floor and set their staff and broom beside the mantle. With one last look at each other, their spirits rejoined with their flesh and they stood feeling the full weight of their bodies again.

They both wiped the slick grease off each other's skin with a damp cloth silently and pulled their clothes back on. As she tied her skirt she finally asked him, "So did we really…? I mean, what happened with us on the mountain top, did that really happen or was it all in my mind?" His lips curled into a devilish smile and through mischievous eyes he looked at her and said, "Yes."

She left his cottage as the dawn crept up the mountainside and made her way towards her home when she heard the window she had snuck in last night unlatch. Her neighbor called out, "Oh, and next time, you're welcome to come in through the front door. See you on the full moon…"

Author's note: This story is inspired by tales of flying to the witches' sabbath. There were many trial records from Scotland, England, Spain, Germany, France, and even America of the infamous witches' sabbath. Many of these records are of course from coerced confessions, but that doesn't change the ways they have affected our craft over the centuries. Folklore about what happened at the sabbath over the centuries has culminated into modern traditional witchcraft.

To this day, practitioners still teach the concept of leaving the body to travel in spirit form to a faraway gathering of witches and the folkloric devil. Many confessions spoke of flying, eating children, and having orgies with the devil. Did that ever happen? Most likely not. Can we as practitioners today still participate in spirit flight and communion with the sabbath on a spiritual plane? Absolutely! We can even do in-person sabbaths that include whatever you feel is comfortable between you and the other attendees. Sex of course is NEVER required and I want to make that very clear. This story includes sex, not as a necessity for initiation, but to push the boundaries of giving into pleasure against societal constraints. Not only that, the order of penetration is reversed to cross that boundary into the realm of transgression and otherworldly experience. Everyone is equal at the sabbath. They are one, even the mysterious figure that brings them together.

4. Our Mother in Red

In a town by the eastern seaboard, beyond a meadow, there once lived a young man named Ilian. He was slender, of average height, and because of his feminine features and delicate demeanor, he was taunted by his family and the townsfolk. He couldn't blame them as he knew it was true. Ever since he was a child, he never felt like a "he". In fact, there were nights when his family was fast asleep that he would put on his sister's silks and dresses. He'd twirl in the gowns feeling the fabric spin around his legs as if they were made for him. He'd lay by the cinders left in the fireplace dreaming of being called by another name. During the day, he avoided the mirror like he'd catch fire if he caught a glimpse of his stubbled face or flat body. Every day was a struggle, and every day, the villagers made sure to remind him.

He liked to escape just outside of town to make flower garlands that would only be worn for a few minutes before leaving them behind to drudge home. He was sitting in a field twisting daisy stems together when a shadow stretched across the flowers in front of him. He quickly hid the garland in his hands but the shadow approached, a silhouette against the sun, and sat down right next to him.

"What pretty flowers," the figure said. Frozen, he sat there unsure of what to do as his eyes focused through the dark reddish haze. He blinked and the figure came into focus. She was a middle-aged woman wearing a scarlet cloak and hood. She smiled at him and said, "By the Old Ones, girl. Put it on. Let me see how pretty you look."

Ilian slowly moved to place the ring of daisies on his head and the woman said, "There now. Don't you make a beautiful queen of the fairies?" Ilian smiled and looked away. The woman scoffed and said slyly with a side-smile, "Well, if the queen will shun me, maybe I'm not welcome?" and pretended to stand, but Ilian quickly grabbed her arm, "Please stay!" he said. "You just surprised me is all. And… no one's ever called me 'she' before… in kindness, I mean."

"Oh pish," said the woman in red. "I know a pretty girl when I see one. I got eyes, don't I? Call me Belinda, at your service!" She nodded her head in an informal introduction. "And you are?"

"Ilian" he replied meekly. "And you're kind, but I know I'm no girl, and I know I'm not pretty," he said with a sigh that let all the air out of his body. "Hmm" Belinda made a sound. "That's not what I see. Here, one moment." She dug through the inner pocket of her crimson cloak and pulled out a small reflective glass.

Handing it to him, Ilian noticed the numerous red, knotted threads on her wrists. He took the handle, also tied in many knots of red thread, and held it up to his face. The sun reflected on it and blinded him for a moment, but then with a slight shift, she saw her face. A sharp inhale of breath escaped Ilian and she looked at Belinda, whose eyes betrayed nothing.

"What is this witchcraft?!" Ilian exclaimed. While terrified, he couldn't put the mirror down. There she was. Her hair was long and oaken with golden flecks of curl. Her lips were pink, her eyes were almond with long lashes. Tears streamed down her face as she saw herself for the first time. Ilian felt for the long hair at his shoulders but it wasn't there, only in the reflection.

"My dear girl, that's exactly what it is. Why do you think I can see what others cannot?" She replied with a cackle. "Why don't you come by my cottage and have some tea with me? I've been spinning all day and could use the company."

Ilian, wary, took one last glance at her reflection in the mirror, then he handed it back to Belinda and in a moment of optimism, he let out a breathy, "Yes."

They made their way over the hill where a sharp pointed roof popped up over the horizon. Ilian had walked this meadow many times but had never seen this cottage before. On the side, there was a wild overgrowth of stalks shooting out rows of leaves in the shape of a star. Red billowing smoke came from the chimney and the front door was split in two, the top half wide open where he could see a fireplace going. "Come in, my pet. I'll warm the kettle," said Belinda.

Ilian entered the cottage under a garland of holly berries and was mesmerized by the trinkets and bottles lining the walls and a large spinning wheel by the fireplace. There was red thread lining the wheel attached to the spindle and there were spools and spools of it in a basket below. There was a work table stained a deep red with what looked like roots from the stalks outside.

"Are those plants bleeding?" Ilian asked wide-eyed. "On no, dear girl. That's madder root. It comes out of the ground like the blood of the earth. It makes a lovely red dye for my spinning," Belinda said. "Sit with me by the fire. Would you?"

They sat in silence for several moments sipping tea till Belinda said, "Well, why don't you get on with it? I can tell your bursting to..." Before she could even finish, Ilian blurted, "Are you really a witch?"

Belinda laughed and said, "Of sorts. I'm a weaver. I weave many things. Sometimes I weave scarves and cloaks, sometimes I weave charms and spells. Like that mirror that you saw your true self in." She crossed her legs exposing little red braids knotted at her ankles. "My true self? What do you mean? That was an illusion wasn't it?" Ilian asked. "No, my dear. That was no illusion, but a glimpse of possible reality," she replied.

"I've been to this meadow many times before. Why have I never seen you or this cottage?" asked Ilian. "I have lived in many places, but I usually show up just when people need me most. Do you think you could use my help, dear girl?" she leaned forward with a quizzical smile.

Ilian sat still in silence, emotions and thoughts running through his head: Memories from childhood being taunted, stolen moments wearing his sister's gowns in the stealth of night, dreaming of being anything other than 'Ilian', the joy he felt seeing herself in the enchanted mirror. Tears started to spill from Ilian's eyes and he said, "How can you help me?"

"Now isn't that the question? First, you must know what you want, my dear. Do you know what it is you want?"

Belinda drew the last question out encouraging Ilian to think.

"I want to be a girl!" Ilian said ever so quietly.

"Darling, I can't make you a girl," she said. Ilian's face fell but she continued, "You already are. Folks just can't see it. Now that's something I think I can help with." Ilian's head shot back up eyes wide. "Really? You can magic a disguise to make me look like a girl?"

"No my dear, I'm going to help you become the woman you are," Belinda said with matter-of-factness. "Come with me." She stood, walked towards the spinning wheel, and pulled out a large spool of thread. Ilian watched as she took the spool to the red-stained work table. She pulled out an old book with lots of ink-stained pages that seemed to have recipes, instructions, and symbols Ilian had never seen before.

Belinda flipped through the pages till she found what she was looking for. "Ah ha! Here it is, a nice all-purpose

transformative. Step forward, girl. Can you write?" She
asked Ilian. "Yes," he replied. She sighed in relief "Good.
This charm packs a punch but requires a few skills. First,
we'll decide the best way to write the spell. These things
can be quite delicate you know. The wording must be
specific. Let's see here. How about:

Present to the world
The truest me
The woman I was always
Meant to be

"Yes, that should do nicely" she admired her rhyme,
unnecessary but it definitely had a ring to it. "Ok, now you
must write the statement from the heart and give it your
breath of life". "Breath of life??" Ilian asked, "what's
that?" "We'll get there, dear. First just write on this bit of
parchment" she replied. Ilian wrote the words feeling his
heart quicken.

"Now hold the note close to your face and breath on it
three times. Each time, feel the words come to life. Give it
your all, dear. This part's the most important. If you don't
mean it, if fear gets in the way, we'll cast ourselves a dud."
She instructed. Ilian held the parchment close to his lips,
closed his eyes, and with his whole body, he let out a
breath from the depths of his soul. The swirling letters
began to glow. "Yes, that's it!" Belinda said with
excitement. "Now, twice more."

Ilian blew twice more and on the final exhale, the letters
glowed so bright the paper began to spark. A flame burst
out of the center and Belinda quickly put an iron plate in

front of Ilian to place the burning petition before his fingers would catch fire.

"What just happened? Did I do something wrong?" he asked. "No no. That was perfect. Now for the second act. Leave the plate with your ashes of desire and sit with me outside." She made her way to the door and they found themselves sitting at an old bench watching the twilight sky shift to night.

They sat there watching the horizon go from dark to light again as the moon rose. "I must say, I'm so glad to have met you on such an evening as this. It's a full moon, and as I said, a time to fully realize your possibilities." Belinda said nonchalantly. "Here. Take this spool and cut 9 strands as long as you can tie to your wrist." Ilian did just that. He cut the 9 strands and waited for further instruction. "Now dearie, with a knot on one end, say under the light of the moon:

By knot of one, this spell's begun

Then break the 9 strands into 3 sets of 3 and begin to braid. As you do, chant:

By mother in red
My words twist and bind
My desire most true
I weave fate's design

You'll repeat that over and over till your nimble fingers meet the threads end."

Ilian looked at her, then the thread in his hands, then up at
the moon. Could this all be real? Could she finally just…
be?

"Go on, dearie. I believe in you." encouraged Belinda. Ilian
looked at her with hope glistening in his eyes one final
time and began to tie the knot.

By knot of one, this spell's begun

He said aloud, and the knot gave him a shock. He jumped
slightly and they both laughed. "Keep going," she
whispered. And he did.

By mother in red
My words twist and bind
My desire most true
I weave fate's design

The thread seemed to become brighter, and Ilian
continued:

By mother in red
My words twist and bind
My desire most true
I weave fate's design

It began to glow:

By mother in red
My words twist and bind
My desire most true
I weave fate's design

The red thread glowed as bright as the moon shown down on them casting a reddish hue across the meadow:

By mother in red
My words twist and bind
My desire most true
I weave fate's design

He continued over and over till the braid came to an end. "Now tie it off and say:"

By knot of two
This spell be true

Ilian did just that and jumped as it sparked and shock him a second time. "Now" continued Belinda, "inside we go before the glow dims. Hurry dear!" They both made their way inside back to the work table where she told Ilian the final steps. "Now spit in the ashes." "Spit?!" He questioned. "Spit, dear. Yes." Ilian shrugged and spit a glob of saliva into what was left of the ashes on the plate from the petition.

"Now mix your spittle with the ash and coat the braid," she told him. Questioning anymore at this point was becoming repetitive so he did as told and watched in amazement as the thread glowing red absorbed the blackened mixture, drinking it up like a traveler in a barren desert. "Now the final touch," Belinda said almost giddy with excitement. "You'll tie the braid around the wrist of your dominant hand." She helped him tie it but instructed, "I may tie, but you must say the final words:"

As it is written
By knot of three
As I will it
So shall it be

Ilian took a breath and the words flowed from his mouth through the air winding with the final knot. The growing crimson light exploded outward. It was so bright, Ilian shut his eyes tight to keep from going blind.

As the glow dimmed, she dared a look back at the charmed braid. There it was. Just a normal bit of embroidery on her delicate wrist. She looked down at herself. She felt her curves and the curls that fell over her shoulders as she turned to face Belinda and the weaver looked back with a mixture of wonder and satisfaction.

Time froze for Ilian. It was as if she were experiencing life for the first time, like being reborn. The fire blazed brighter. The night air smelled sweeter. The crickets' song more melodic than ever. *"How did I ever live before today?"* she thought.

"There you are," Belinda said as if clearly seeing Ilian for the first time. "Now the world can see the truth of you," she continued. "What about the town? What about my family?" Ilian asked. "They will know you as you've always been, a spirited girl with a penchant for long walks in the meadow and a love of head garlands," Belinda said back as she placed the ring of daisies atop her head.

They made their way to the entryway and said their goodbyes. As she walked a few paces from the front door, Belinda called out, "Oh, and Iliana!". She stopped. Iliana. That was her name. She turned having envisioned this moment for as long as she could remember. The top half of the door was still open with Belinda looking like a portrait perfectly centering the square frame. "You should know" Belinda continued, "Only a witch could wield that spell. I have a feeling we'll meet again. I may have something for you. Something in red I think." Her words echoed over the hill leaving Iliana overwhelmed with the events of the evening. As she walked back towards town, she turned one last time to wave goodbye, but when she did, she was facing nothing but an empty meadow of daisies and a haze of red chimney smoke.

*For more on the origin of this story, reference the final section in part I, Cunning Tales.

Authors note: In all my years, I've never come across a fairytale that gave voice to the Trans experience. While this is of course a fantasy and I know magic cannot transform one's gender, it certainly would drastically reduce the hardships many trans people experience in their lifetime. Was the woman in red an older version of Iliana encouraging her past self? Was Belinda trans? Is this an entire story about how inherently queer witchcraft is? As a queer person, I often think about what I would say to my younger self, and I like to believe I would do what I could to erase the hardships I went through, but I know that would be a fantasy. Iliana got to have her fairytale and for the first time, she was recognized and respected for who she was. That's a happy ending I think we all deserve.

I'd like to thank my friends Mhara and Krystal for reading this story and providing feedback as to include the trans voice. As a gay man, coming to terms with my own gender fluidity has been quite the journey and I'm grateful to be surrounded by a diverse and inclusive group of people.

5. Our Mother in Green

There once was a cliffside village that looked over the North Sea. The town was triangular in shape: one side backed up to the rickety cliffs, one side to a dark forest, and the third to an open road that led miles to the next town over. It was a small but bustling community, and within its confines lived a myriad of folk.

At a point near where the forest met the cliffside, there was an old ramshackle of a home. Just a few rooms for Vivyanne, a mother, and her two children, Inka and Vix. Vivyanne was a midwife to the town and healer. She kept a garden of herbs known to spirit away illness, soothe a fever, and stop blood in its tracks.

When a fever broke out in the village, it was Vivyanne who took her feverfew and lemon balm elixir to each of the homes of the afflicted. When the local butcher cut his finger and it became infected, it was Vivyanne's aloe, clove, and oregano salve along with instructions to wash 3 times daily with lye soap that saved his finger and possibly his life. When the town minister's wife had a breached birth, it was Vivyanne who successfully turned the baby to deliver her child safely.

One day, a wagon carrying a pinched man and his sour wife pulled into town. He announced he was a doctor and had arrived to provide his services as he has heard that this town was lacking the presence of any medical care.

The villagers were grateful to have a doctor in town for it was growing and Vivyanne couldn't keep up even with the help of her two children. The Doctor was informed of the Healer but he scoffed at her old herbal potions calling them "poppycock." He assured the townsfolk now that a real doctor was here, the use of fairy medicine would be a thing of the past.

The day his doors opened, he saw patient after patient. He moved swiftly through them using leeches to bleed out their sickness and a new quicksilver cure for lesions and boils. He took away their pain with milk of the poppy and they were glad.

 Vivyanne saw what this learned doctor was doing and offered advice on cleanliness to help stop the spread of illness. He scoffed and threw the lye soap back at her. "How dare you presume to advise me, you witch!" Stunned into silence, she retreated surprised at his vitriol.

Soon she found herself being called upon by the doctor's patients. Dazed, they arrived at her door weak with blood loss and delirious from his poppy pain elixirs no better than before. She got to work quickly going home to home offering what she could for those who would have her. Some threw her out having listened to this new doctor no matter his shortcomings as an actual healer.

Wearing her black hooded cloak, she daily went through the village offering aid to those who wasted away. The quicksilver drove many mad and they became paranoid about her visits.

"Could the doctor be right?"

"Was Vivyanne taking revenge on the villagers who forsook her help?"
Many went back to the doctor again and again for more of his pain elixirs and he happily kept them appeased.

More whispers spread of Vivyanne peddling maladies rather than remedies. The Doctor thrived from these rumors and even added to them.

"I can only imagine since my arrival she is jealous of my success. She is no healer, she's a charlatan witch!"

Many long-time friends of Vivyanne and her children rallied around them but doubt crept through the town like a poisonous fog. When the Doctor's patients started to die, he blamed Vivyanne for their deaths.

"It was her who glided through town cursing all who crossed her path," he said. The elixir-intoxicated towns folk, so pliant, listened. The wild ravings of syphilitics, mad from the mercury shouted for vengeance.

Nearby villagers loyal to Vivyanne found her by the forest collecting herbs. They told her of the crowd gathering into a mob all looking for her. She turned as the sound of their shouts became audible and they spotted her by the tree line. Her friends tried to calm them but the mob was riled and hysterical. She dropped her basket of herbs and ran. She ran along the forest's edge, her black cloak flowing behind her. Her children Inka and Vix watched from the window as their mother ran towards their home.

Vivyanne knew she couldn't just run inside. Her children were in there. The mob would end them all. Then, she saw the cliff's edge and knew a decision had to be made.

Her children watched as she ran towards the point. She ran past the house along the tree line toward the edge of the cliff. They watched as she looked back at them, her eyes saying so much more than eyes should be able to say.

The mob saw her in the distance as she ran past her house. Vivyanne's friends slowed, confused, *Where was she going?* Then, they abruptly stopped and gasps cut through the air.

Vivyanne jumped. She ran right past the last tree to the very edge… and leaped.

The mob regained their wits and rushed to the edge. They looked over and her friends screamed as they saw Vivyanne's black cloak wash up against the rocks.

She was gone...

Or was she?

Her children had watched through the window as the mob in the distance ran along the tree line towards their home where the forest boundary and the cliff met. They watched their mother as she ran towards the edge and gave them a knowing look. They watched as she grabbed the final tree at the cliff's end with her right hand, and threw her cloak over the edge with her left. She swung her body around the other side of the tree and swiftly ran deep into the woods. They watched as the crowd made their way to the edge, but by the time they arrived, their mother was gone.

That night, she stealthily made her way back to her cottage where her children were waiting for her. She told them of her plan to relocate to the woods but she'd need their help.

Under the light of the full moon, they picked the garden clean of all greenery. In a boiling pot, they boiled the Lemon balm, Feverfew, Mugwort, Sage, Yarrow, and Shepards Purse till the water was a deep green. Then they threw in the largest bolt of wool cloth they owned and watched as it soaked up the brew, eventually becoming a deep shade of emerald.

"With this green cloak as my disguise, I shall blend into the woods. The better I can keep watch over my darlings and never be far should you need me." She continued, "The villagers will realize their wrongs and when they do, they will come back here and we will help them. We are healers. It's what we do."

Time passed. The "Doctor" and his wife packed up and slipped away in the night as they knew with every death under their care, the tide was turning against them. Friends and villagers found their way back to Vivyanne's doorstep where Inka and Vix took them in. They used what was left from the regrowing garden to do what they could, but for the tough cases, they lit a green candle in the window. At nightfall, their mother would come from the woods at the candlelight's signal covered by the night sky and her forest green cloak.

Tales of their mother's ghost coming from the woods or flying down from the sky to heal the sick made their way through town. People would find reasons to go to the point and search the clouds or watch for glimpses of movement just inside the forest's edge. They made songs about her healing magic and emerald cloak.

Many miraculous things arose from that house. Visitors and those who needed help would seek the cottage and the company of The Green Mother. As time moved on, Vivyanne passed down her cloak to Inka, then Inka to Vix. Years came and went, and with them, so did Vivyanne followed by her daughters…but their legacy lived on.

The garden grew wild spreading clear to the cliff's edge, and every year the villagers would come and collect the healing herbs when needed. They picked sprigs of lemon balm, yarrow, feverfew, mugwort, sage, and shepherd's purse, and they would sing the rhymes their parents had taught them.

Lady viridian
Veiled in chartreuse
Lend me your aid
All ailments reduce
By spirits of earth
May you intervene
Affliction begone
Dear Mother in green

And every now and then, a few villagers would come back from the garden and swear they saw a green-cloaked figure disappear into the woods.

*For more on the origin of this story, reference the final section in part I, Cunning Tales.

6. Damned Devil's Berries

Tessa, a young servant to a wealthy mistress, was sent out to the forest to pick wild strawberries one dewy morning. She always woke up before the sun rose, her days spent caring for a demanding mistress. Any chore that got her out of the house was a blessing. Sometimes

she would even get to see a few of the other servants in the village. They traded gossip, recipes, and even horrific stories of their lords and ladies.

Her Mistress had taken to enjoying fresh wild strawberries on Sundays after church. So almost every Sunday, Tessa missed services to scavenge the woods for fresh ripened red berries. She didn't mind though. Sitting and listening to the old monotone minister had become awfully boring over the years.

She would put on her wool cloak to protect her from the brisk morning air, and with her basket, she'd make her way deep into the forest. The trick was finding patches of the berries before the birds did. They were responsible for spreading the seeds with their droppings but also for eating the majority of them too. "Tricky little devil," Tessa mused, as she saw a yellow bird watching her efforts. She gathered enough for her mistress's breakfast and made her way back home.

At the breakfast table sat the sharp-angled woman waiting eagerly for her dish when Tessa brought in the bowl of washed shiny red berries and a side of fresh whipped cream.

"There you are, you lazy girl!" She harrumphed.

"Sorry ma'am," Tessa replied, "The berries seem to disagree with the season and I searched all morning to find these."

"Well, next week you'll have to start earlier or expect a beating, girl" spat the mistress.

The next week, Tessa walked into the woods before first light. She was determined to avoid one of Madam's lashings. She often lost her temper if Tessa didn't cry enough, and she knew by the smile and beaded brow how much the Lady enjoyed it. It could be worse. The horrors of the cruel lords some of the other servants had shared made her lady's lashings seem minuscule.

"Oh not you again," Tessa sighed as she saw the yellow bird watching her search. "You're the reason I'm out searching so early for these damned devil's berries."

The light was just breaking over the horizon when she heard a deep voice. "Damned devil's berries... how delightful."

She turned swiftly, aghast at the deep yet soft voice, but when she looked, she saw nothing but trees, bushes, and that pestering yellow bird. "Is someone there?" She whispered, visibility shaken.

"Are you looking for these, Tessa?" The velvet voice spoke again and she turned.

There was a man, a young, wealthy-looking man wearing a yellow wide-brim hat and waist-length cloak with a matching suit. He had on gold buckled shoes, a shiny black cane, a gold pocket watch, and small circular glasses tinted a shade of amber. He was truly a sight to see, bright as the sun in the still-dark and dreary forest.

"Beg your pardon, sir," Tessa bowed her head. "How did you know my name?"

The man ignored her question and instead asked again, "Are you looking for these?" He stood aside and behind him was a large patch of beautiful bright red ripened strawberries.

"Yes!" She exclaimed with glee.

"I'd be happy to share them with you if you sit for a moment and enjoy the dawn with me," he replied.

Warily, she moved forward and he pulled a small yellow pillow from behind his back. "Where did that come from?" she gasped.

"It's a gift. Here, have a seat next to me," he said as he flipped a switch on his cane and it swung open into a small stool on three legs.

She took the pillow and sat down by the strawberry patch, now having to look up at him perching on the stool. The sky above was only beginning to lighten so she knew her mistress would still have to rise and go to services before she'd be expecting Tessa.

"Sir, how did you know my name?"

"You must have told it to me I'm sure," he said smoothly, "I've seen you in my woods a time or two stealing… what did you call them, 'damned devil's berries'?"

"Oh, sir I apologize! I didn't realize this was your land. I'm so sorry," Tessa bowed her head in remorse.

"My sweet maiden," said the man, "you may come as often as you like. My lands are vast but only visited by those most cunning." This statement made no sense to Tessa but it would be rude to question such a kind offer.

"Go ahead. Pick your fill for your mistress. Quickly, before the birds get them" he said through a sly grin.

She started gathering the berries, then stopped. She had not spoken of her mistress or her reason for foraging. "Sir," she said as she turned but jumped with fright as the man was now sitting on the other side of her as if he'd been there the whole time.

"Will you not take a few for yourself?" he asked.

"Oh no, that would be no good of me", Tessa said as she picked the last berry. "My mistress would have my hide if she knew."

"Then we shan't tell her, shall we?" the man in yellow replied as he pulled out one last blood-red, ripe, shining berry.

It was so shiny she could almost see her reflection in the flesh of the fruit. Her mouth began to water knowing how sweet it would taste. She hesitantly took it into her palms. She hadn't tasted a strawberry in years, not since the first one her mistress caught her stealing. That lashing had turned the memory sour as the pain wretched it back up with bile.

She sat there now agonizing over one single berry. "I have a thought," said the man interrupting Tessa's inner turmoil. "This delectable berry can be just for you and I'll offer you another to replace it for your mistress."

Tessa looked around at the now picked-over patch. "I see no others, sir."

"I know where some others grow, but these berries are special. They're magic," he told her.

"Really?! What do they do?" She asked, more curious than ever.

"I'll tell you only if I can tempt you with the one I offer. Go on, it will spoil if you don't. You know there's nothing as sweet as a strawberry before it turns." He looked at her calmly with an almost golden gleam in his eyes.

She held the berry in her palm and brought it to her lips. She could smell its sweetness as it slid under her nose and the rough yet soft flesh of the fruit brushed her lips. She looked at him directly in the eyes through the amber-tinted glasses and took a bite.

An explosion of saccharine juice filled her mouth. The tartness caused her eyes to roll back into her head. What was this feeling of ecstasy causing her head to throw back and moan at the deliciousness of this fruit? How could one berry send waves of pleasure over her body? She didn't care as she took a second bite and the sun lifted from the horizon shining down over the morning dew. Everything sparkled. Her head flew back again and again, as gasps escaped her glistening lips. She laid back, her toes tingling, slowly glowing with sweat and breathlessness.

"What was that?" She asked speaking through heaving breaths.

"That, my dear, is the sweet taste of power," he said in almost a whisper so close to her ears she moaned again reveling in the memory.

"I want more," she said through the afterglow.

"More I shall bestow upon you, sweet Tessa," he replied, "but first, come with me."

She stood feeling lightheaded and slowly began to follow his golden presence. It was strange. The forest looked different. The sounds were louder. The colors were more vibrant. The birdsongs were more whimsical, all except for the little yellow bird who seemed to have gone missing.

A few minutes later they arrived at a large bushel. It had large velvety leaves, white trumpet-like flowers, and a fruit of some kind that was green and covered in spikes. "That's the fruit you expect me to swap out for a strawberry?!" she asked incredulously.

"I do," he said with a mischievous grin, "watch." He took one of the spiny pods and plucked it from its stem. He held it in the palm of his hand and said, "spit on it."

"Spit?!" Tessa replied surprised.

"Yesssss," he said in a whisper that faded into a serpent-like hiss. "Trussst me. Spit on it and hold out your hand."

Still feeling full of newness and excitement, she spat on the ugly sharp fruit in his hand and held out her own palm up. He closed his gloved fingers around it and placed it in her palm. When he removed his hand, a shiny deep red strawberry sat there, dewy and glistening in the now rising sun. "Oh, my heavens!" Tessa exclaimed.

"Not quite," the man said in return. "Now add this to the plate of berries for your crude mistress. When she gets to this one, it will stick in her throat and as long as it stays there, she won't be able to speak or act without your say-so."

"What?! Oh no! I couldn't do that! That would make me wicked!" She backed away only to bump into the yellow man now standing behind her.

"Not wicked, my dear Tessa. Powerful, as powerful as your mistress. Powerful enough to stop her from beating you. Powerful enough to stop her wickedness!" He said, with each word more enticing.

Tessa stood there for a moment. She never in her wildest dreams had considered a life free from fear, free from captivity, free from the tyranny of her mistress. That was the moment she looked up from the berry in her palm and chose herself. She turned to face the man but he was gone, nowhere to be seen. There was just a little yellow bird flapping near the branches of the large bushel. She looked at its golden eyes for one very long moment, turned, and made her way home.

Walking from the kitchen with the plate of strawberries in her hand and a bowl of fresh whipped cream in the other, she entered the dining room where her mistress waited impatiently. "Finally," she exclaimed, "I've been waiting all morning!" She set the plate on the table, her hand shaking as she did. She had forgotten which berry on the plate was *the* berry. "*I guess we'll find out together,*" Tessa thought to herself.

The wicked mistress took a bite of the first fruit, then the second, then the third. Nothing. A fourth, a fifth, a sixth, seventh, eighth, and finally at the ninth one, she bit off the entire berry and became very still. Her eyes widened. Tessa looked on in fear but her excitement was beginning to quicken. Her mistress gasped trying to cough, but nothing would come out. She stared at Tessa, eyes watering. "What have you done?" they seemed to plead.

Tessa began to laugh. It surprised her. Deep down she was afraid it might not work but now in the moment of fruition, she laughed. It was laughter that came from relief, relief from the burden she had been carrying for as long as she could remember. As she laughed louder and more fervently the same waves of pleasure began coursing through her body. Again, she felt breathless. She became overwhelmed with hysterics as if all the weight she'd been carrying was suddenly lifted away.

She took the plate of strawberries and sat down next to the now docile, tear-streaked, mute woman. She dipped one in cream and ate it slowly. Thoughts of what to do next surged through her mind. So many ideas and so much time, time she never had before. Time to say and do what her heart desired.

"Fetch me some wine!" she commanded. The mute woman now stood and walked to the sidebar. She poured a heaping glass of red wine and brought it to Tessa in a golden goblet. She sipped and walked towards her balcony overlooking the landscape, her landscape.

The sun rose over the forest trees and a birdsong caught her ears. "Hello again, yellow bird", she said to him as he flew inside landing on the ground in gold buckled shoes,

"Welcome to my home," Tessa told him with a prideful grin. She beckoned to the once cruel mistress to bring forth the plate. "May I offer you a strawberry?" She offered the handsome young man now standing before her, glowing in gold and yellow hues.

He opened his mouth ever so slightly and she picked up the last ripe red glistening fruit. She placed it between his lips and a wave of heat soared through her once more. He bit, and she smiled with pleasure. "Is this what wickedness feels like?" Tessa asked him.

"No, my sweet. This is what freedom feels like," he replied. "Tell me, Tessa, what will you do with your newfound sovereignty?"

She seemed to think for a few moments and looked up at the man's golden eyes. "What does freedom mean if it only belongs to me?" she said. "I believe sir, I'd like to introduce you to a few friends."

Author's note: In April of 2022, I visited Salem, Massachusetts, and while on a walking tour, I was inspired by the story of Tituba. Tituba was enslaved by the Salem Village minister Samuel Parris, and taken from her home in Barbados. Treated as a scapegoat for a group of young girls who claimed to be bewitched, she was accused of being in league with the devil and was beaten to coerce a confession. She told a tall tale of meeting the devil in the forest and signing her name in his book. She said he had familiars with him which included a hog, a black dog, a cat, and a little yellow bird. She was the first to be accused in 1692, and although she wasn't a witch, she was quite cunning. She told them she could see other names in the book and even gave two of them, Sarah Osborne and Sarah Good. She was clever and claimed she couldn't quite make out the other names, but if they gave her time, she'd try to recall them. She was never sentenced and remained imprisoned for over a year before the trials ended. At that time, prisoners were charged for their food and stay in the jails, so many went deep into debt just waiting for their trials behind bars. Her case was dismissed in May of 1693 by a grand jury and eventually, Samuel Parris sold Tituba to another enslaver who paid off her debt. It is tragically unknown what came of her afterward.

7. The Three Wise Healers

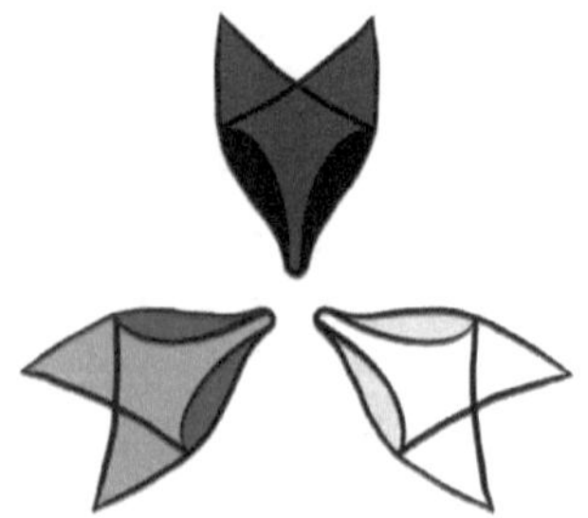

"Grandma, tell me the story again," said the little boy all snug and tucked in bed.

"Again?" Asked the old woman. "Alright, let's see now..."

"There once were 3 wise healers. One with hair as red as blood, one as black as a raven, and one as fair as flax. The first healed your wounds. The second took your pain, and the third made you whole again."

"No. No. No! Not there! Tell the whole story!" cried the young boy.

"Ahh. You want a tale then. Ok, let's see. Where to start..."

In a great castle on the northeastern coast, there once lived a beautiful Queen who was married to a loving King. One day, they both came down with a sickness. First came the fever which was followed by a ghastly pox.

None would enter their chambers for fear of catching their illness. As the days went by, they grew weaker and weaker. Wounds boiled up all over their skin and they lay there thinking of the lives they would never have for they were sure to die.

The king eventually succumbed to the fever breaking the queen's heart. Weeks went by as she waited for death but fate had something different in store for her.

One evening she opened up the tower windows and shouted to the blackened sky, "Take me night! Take me into your embrace." The wind howled and blew her back. She fell onto her bed and deep into a feverish dream.

She awoke in the middle of the night. Her window was still open and the moon was high reflecting off the ocean. She lay there listening.

Scratch, scratch, scratch.

What had awoken her?

Scratch, scratch, scratch.

It was coming from the window. She sat up just in time to see a fox crawling through. It came closer and pounced on her bed. It was a deep burnt orange with a red muzzle as crimson as blood. It crept closer but she felt unafraid. No one had come to see her since the sickness had taken them, but this fox, this fox was welcome company.

It stepped closer, its paws making soft indentions in the silk bedding. The Queen laid back as it curled up on her lap pressing its paws into her chest. She breathed deeply and relished the comforting touch.

One by one, the red oozing pustules slowly began to shrink. The lesions weeping their foul fluid dried and every pox mark on her body faded away.

At first, she didn't realize what was happening as she still felt the pain in her muscles and weakness from the fever. That's when she heard the second set of paws. She looked towards the window as a sleek black fox slipped in. It crawled up on the banister of the foot of her bed and she saw its fur was as black as the night sky. "Oh, what a treat!" She exclaimed. "Two visitors in one night!"

The second fox hopped forward and as it got closer and closer she looked into its eyes. They were deep obsidian and reflective as glass. She felt the pain leave her body the same moment she saw her pox-free face in the reflection of the foxes knowing eyes. "Dear sweet creature of darkness, how you've come on the evening I needed you most!"

She gasped in relief. It had been weeks of agony with no reprieve. She had felt as if she'd turn to stone with how rigid her muscles had felt and she breathed with ease though still a bit weak. A laugh escaped her throat and she smiled "This must be a dream," she said aloud as she saw the final creature hop into her chamber.

It was so quick she almost missed it as it was just a white furry blur. A fox as stark as snow glided in, its nose and whiskers twitched as if to acknowledge her with a "good evening, madam." She began to feel a bit delirious with now with three foxes all sitting on her lap in bed. How had they even gotten up here in the castle tower window?

The white fox inched forward closer and closer. She laid back as it came up to her face and sat nose to nose. The whiskers twitched again tickling her face and neck. The tickle quickly became something more, a tingle, a wave of weight slowly lifted off of her as if a blanket of illness had been removed.

She sat up in amazement. She jumped from the bed and danced with joy twirling under the moonlight shining in her window. She thought her end had come but instead, the night had brought her something different.

She eventually fell asleep warm in bed, the red, black, and white foxes all curled up together in her lap. When she awoke, they were gone. At first, she thought it must have been a dream but realized the sores and her pain had vanished.

She jumped from her bed and ran to the still-open window. She peered out and breathed in the fresh sea air. "Where ever you are, kind beasts, thank you," she called out to the dawn. She left her room for the first time in over a month and made her way down to the throne room. There, her mother-in-law sat on the throne with a disdainful look on her face.

"My goodness," the matron gasped. "Your majesty, you're… well?"

"Yes", the Queen replied.

"It was the most miraculous recovery!" She recounted her tale of the three beasts to the Matron and the entire court listened with bated breath. She told them of the three foxes. She told them how they came through her window in the night. She told them of how they took her wounds, her pain, and made her whole again.

The court chattered in amazement and they were all so happy to have their Queen back. Well, almost all of them. The wicked mother-in-law who had been the power-hungry stepmother to the former king thought to herself, *"I finally had the opportunity to rule and this wretched woman escapes the brink of death to come snatching the crown right back off my head."*

"Poppycock!" The wicked woman's voice echoed through the great hall. "Guards, arrest this woman. Only a deal with the devil could escape the same illness that killed our great king! Only a Witch would call upon familiar beasts of the night to take her woes and not our kings too! Lock her in the dungeon. She is queen no more!"

The Queen sat locked in the dungeon for weeks. With her crown stolen, there was no one left to rule but her wicked Mother-in-Law. No trial was set. No sentence was given. She waited and waited and as she did, her belly grew. Months went by and soon even the new wicked Queen Mother knew she couldn't ignore the rumors of the town's people.

"I hear the Queen is pregnant with the King's child!"

"How can the King's own mother keep her future grandchild in such squaller?"

"I'll bet she locked away the Queen so she can keep the throne all to herself."

The wicked woman knew she had to think fast and unfortunately, she soon found a way to twist fate in her favor.

It was dusk when the real Queen's water broke. She screamed and pushed as the midwife helped to deliver the next heir. The baby was born and a gasp rang out from the ladies as the child was revealed to have hair as red as blood. A second child was born seconds later and this child had hair as black as a raven. A minute went by and finally, a third child was born, this one having hair as fair as flax.

She had given birth to three beautiful girls and she lay there with all three safely wrapped in her lap crying in relief. That relief was short-lived though as her Mother-in-Law learned of the three children who looked nothing like the tall and handsome king with hair the color of chestnuts.

The wicked Mother-in-Law saw an opportunity. "These aren't my son's heirs! These are the babes of the devil's whore!" She proclaimed. "She has given me no choice. Tomorrow, she and her beastly spawn are to be burned at the stake. Guards! Prepare the kindling!"

The midwife who had helped to birth the children and saw the three tiny babes with their hair of red, black, and white knew they were special. So in the darkness of night, with no moon in the sky, the midwife secreted the Queen and her three babies out of the castle. She held them close and they slept soundly the whole way never making a peep.

She took them deep into the woods heading west and there they met with a shadowy figure. The figure was cloaked in a deep green cape and she seemed older but quite nimble. The midwife whispered to the old woman in green and then stood back. The woman walked forward and pulled back her hood. She was older yes but with eyes the color of emeralds. She looked careworn but strength still emanated from her voice.

"You may call me Vivyanne," she said. "The midwife has told me of your tale young Queen. She tells me that spirits of my woods have visited you and brought you a great blessing." She looked down at the three infants sleeping soundly in the queen's arms. "Come. You may stay in my cottage with my children."

The midwife left and they followed the woman called Vivyanne till the sun began to rise. They came out the other side to a cottage by a cliff. Dawn was brightening the dim sky and she could make out a large garden on the sides of a wooden and stone house with a steeply pointed roof. Two middle-aged women called Inka and Vix came out to help them. Vivyanne then left them there and spirited herself back to the woods and the Queen didn't see her again for years.

Back at the castle, the wicked Mother-in-Law watched as the kindling was lit at the stake in the center of the city. She sipped wine and smiled as the face of the queen and her three screaming babes went up in flames. In fact, she had enjoyed so much wine, she hadn't even seen the tiny red braid around the burning queen's wrist. If she had, she would have known it wasn't the queen, but the very midwife who had given her life to help the queen escape.

It was a simple spell, one of transformation she had learned from a weaver she met once who taught her a bit of transformation magic. The drunk wicked Mother-in-Law didn't even see the red braid burn off transforming the burning Queen back into the midwife holding three squealing piglets. She laughed believing herself to be victorious and declared herself the Matron Queen of the kingdom.

Years went by and the true Queen raised her three children in the cottage with the two spinster sisters. It was a happy life tending the garden and aiding the sisters in their craft as healers of the cliffside village.

They grew to be young ladies beautiful and fair. They were taught the art of healing and herbs, but Inka and Vix knew the girls' gifts would far surpass theirs and the day had come for their mother to return.

The full moon rose and the Green Mother glided out of the woods and to their back door. She sat with the Queen and her girls and told them of three legendary spirits.

"You see my Queen, the
first spirit was the spirit of
blood and had the power
to heal all wounds. The
second was a spirit of the
void that would banish all
pain. The third, the spirit
of purity had the gift to
make one feel whole
again. They were old, so
old they couldn't even
change forms anymore.

"Years ago, I came across their path. They told me they
were on their way to perform one last miracle before they
died. A miracle to be sure their gifts would pass on."

Realization began to come over the Queen as she looked at
her girls and she remembered that fateful night so many
years ago. It had been no dream but the last sacrificial act
of three wise spirits.

The woman in green continued, "When I saw your three
babes in the woods that night, I knew they carried these
spirits as you know now."

The girls hugged their mother and she remembered how
quickly she had healed after giving birth to three children
and still been able to escape death-defying odds only hours
later. It seems they had been gifted since birth… or
possibly long before.

One day weeks later, there was a shout outside the cottage. "Help! Please I need help," cried a desperate woman carrying her young son. "Inka, Vix, please," she begged.

They brought them into the cottage and laid the boy on the table. He was bleeding from an arrow wound in his chest, barely breathing, almost lifeless. "He was shot by the wicked queen's huntsman as they mistook him for a fawn." Crying, she heaved herself to the floor begging through sobs for them to save her precious son.

Inka glanced at her sister's face and through pitiful frowns, they looked back at the sobbing woman. "This may be beyond us, my lady". The woman cried, desperate for anything that would save her son.

"What if… what if we could help," said the red-haired maiden as she and her two sisters stepped forward.

"Anything please anything!!!" cried the desperate mother.

They walked forward and the red-haired sister placed her hands atop the wound and closed her eyes. She envisioned the blood stopping, the wound closing up, and the arrow retracting from the body leaving behind clean smooth unmarked skin. There was a gasp from the room as she opened her eyes to see the arrow laying on the boy's chest not a drop of blood in sight.

He still lay unmoving, and the sister with hair the color of blackness stepped forward. She placed her hands on the boy and gasped. She could feel the pain the boy was in. She could feel the shock and trauma of being shot so violently, but as soon as she felt it, it slipped away. Like water through her fingers, it washed away with her touch.

The sister with hair as fair as flax stepped forward and placed her hands on the boy and without missing a moment his eyes opened. "Mama?" He said weakly. And the woman cried in relief as she hugged her young son. The Queen looked at her daughters in amazement. Her children were magic.

It didn't take long for the villagers to hear of the three healing sisters and as they grew so did their gifts. Vivyanne came at least once a month under the light of the moon and taught them the healing power of touch and medicine in the plants of the land.

One day she stopped coming and they knew she had joined the spirits of the woods. They had children and expanded the cottage to fit more rooms and the garden blossomed to accommodate the large household. People would travel from distant kingdoms to pay homage and ask for help from the sisters. They had become so well known, they were now called the Three Wise Healers. Where they and their magic had come from, nobody else knew.

Inka and Vix, now old, acted as grand aunts to the sisters, and with their mother, the true Queen, they lived happily as a family for many years.

"There now my grandsons, are you satisfied?" The old woman telling the story asked.

The boy looked at his brothers next to him in their triplet beds. "Yes, grandma! Goodnight!" they said in unison.

She looked at her grandsons, each with hair of red, black, and white, before blowing out the candle. Her own red hair had faded long ago but it was no matter. It wasn't lost, only passed down. She gave each of them a kiss on the cheek.

"Good night, my little foxes."

Epilogue

Far away, through a dark forest, in the tower of her stolen castle, the Wicked Matron Queen had heard of three girls living in a village not far. She had heard of their gifts and more importantly, the color of their hair. *Could they be the three babes she had burnt so long ago?* she thought to herself. She made a mental note to look into it in the morning as she sipped the wine she always enjoyed before bed.

It wasn't till she finished the goblet that she saw the macerated berries stuck to the bottom. She swallowed as she recognized them for their deadly beauty and looked up to see the shadow of a woman holding a forked staff cloaked all in black with a hood obscuring her face.

"Who are you?" The wicked Matron Queen's words stumbled out in fear.

"It's no matter. You won't live long enough to remember my name," answered the woman in a velvet voice.

The wicked Matron Queen looked as if she was about to respond but the words stuck in her throat and her head fell to the table, the dead weight it now was.

The woman cloaked in black smiled, took her staff, and flew out the tower window just as if she'd never been there at all.

Author's note: Several years ago, I came across a beautiful piece of photographic art by Anastasiya Dobrovolskaya. It was an image of three women holding three foxes. One was red, one was black, and one was white. It was so striking I saved the image and would look at it on my phone over and over. My mind was entranced by these three figures. I knew something more was there. It first led me to write a narrative charm in the fall of 2021, followed by a full spell as seen in Part III, chapter 11.

There once were 3 wise healers.
One with hair as red as blood
One as black as a raven
And one as fair as flax
The first healed your wound
The second took your pain
And the third made you whole again

I knew there was more to their story. Who were they? Where did they come from? What's the origin of their magic?

Their tale came to me in the summer of 2022. My city in Texas had a large outbreak of monkeypox. As a queer man living in the heart of the "gayborhood", I was surrounded by friends who became infected and went for weeks in isolation. Texas was moving very slowly to cooperate with the federal government for aid. Politicians used this new "plague" to divisively target gay men as it was at the time predominantly spreading amongst us. We only finally received vaccine access once the pox had spread to several cases in children. Queer people came together and signed up to stop the spread of this pox. We lined up in our cars for hours waiting at drive-through vaccination sites. Within months, the spread had slowed drastically, and by January of 2023, very few cases were reported.

I spoke the original chant (from 2021) over a charm I made for my friend who was infected. He was on day 10 of isolation and I dropped it off at his doorstep. He wore the charm and within days his pox began to dry up. His body ache began to fade and he started to feel better. This is how the tale of the Three Wise Healers came to be.

8. Our Mother in Black

Oliviana sat on the pub balcony sipping her tea. She had just returned from a mission with great success and wanted to treat herself. She cut into the slice of cake before her and let the sweet crumbly bite melt on her tongue.

She was one of the few female assassins in the surrounding kingdoms and felt a sense of pride about that. Her skill with knives was beyond reproach and she had a unique ability to get into tough-to-reach spaces.

A few years back, she had run into a couple who had gifted her an ointment that allowed her spirit to glide upon the currents of the wind. No other assassin could have flown out of the tower window she had, her actual body hidden miles away.

But her greatest skill was in poisons. Belladonna, Datura, Bindweed, Mandrake, and stinging nettle were her specialties. From poison darts to pies and wines, she had rid the world of those she deemed most vile.

First, there was her uncle who snuck into her room at night when she was a child. She baked him a meat pie with a spicy jam made from blueberry, raspberry, and belladonna. She found him the next morning blue in the face and frozen stiff with a look of horror in his eyes. She knew she'd found her calling.

Then there was the town sheriff who was extorting the local charity house. She knew he frequented the brothel on Knight street so she waited there to entice him. Once his pants were down she stabbed his jugular with a porcupine needle coated in a concentration of poisons. At first, he fell to the ground in the alleyway paralyzed and unable to move. "I think this time, it's you who deserves a little prick," she said to him and pulled out her full case of needles and began to work her art.

They found him later that day, bloated and stuck with spines all over his body. His eyes were empty, and mouth agape.

Then there was the doctor who had fled a nearby village after poisoning the townsfolk with mercury and creating a slew of poppy addicts. She took a job as a cook at the public house he and his wife were hiding out in. She made him a special stew from the very mercury he had stowed away in his room. He went mad in a matter of days and was burned after offending the royal house.

That's when her attention turned to the Queen. She had heard that the monarch had burned her own daughter-in-law and three grandchildren just to keep her crown. *A perfect mark* Oliviana thought to herself. That night she glided out of the queen's tower with the most satisfying feeling.

She finished her last sip of tea and polished off her plate, stood up, and walked towards her ramshackle homestead where the forest met the swamps.

Unfortunately, she wasn't alone.

She followed the stream from the forest's edge into the depths to meet an area that softened to become a bog. This and the stinging nettle that surrounded the area usually kept anyone from lurking about. There was a clearing where sunlight still peaked through to bring life to her garden and home built of stone and mortar so as to not rot and slip into the swamp.

She blew a kiss to her beautiful poisonous plants. The shiny black berries of the belladonna swayed back as if welcoming her home. The datura had grown so large its branches had crept into her side window to bloom in the shade. Its thorny seed pods were ripe and ready for Oliviana to harvest. The bindweed crawled up one whole side of the dwelling covered in vines of green leaves and white and purple flowers.

She made a fire in the small hearth and sat in her old rocking chair. Unfortunately, the floorboards didn't creak till the blade was at her throat and the woman holding it behind her said, "you killed my husband, you Witch!" The woman slid the knife across Oliviana's throat and she gagged on the blood that immediately rushed out of her now gaping neck.

She had only a few moments to stand, turn, and take in the intruder. She recognized her right away from the public house as the wife of the doctor whom she had driven mad with his own mercury. She gurgled trying to say something, but only blood came up.

She collapsed on the floor bleeding out in front of the fireplace. The woman still holding the knife cut down a few bundles of drying herbs and tossed them atop Oliviana's body for kindling. Then she took a large jar of grain alcohol from the kitchen and walked towards the front door. She stood there and looked back at the poisoner she had just murdered, tossed the jar towards the fireplace, and left.

"Die, you bitch," she muttered as the explosion of flames ignited behind her.

Oliviana lay there, the flames blistering her skin. She should have died, but the bundle of drying herbs had other ideas. The blackberries instead burst in the heat, and their juice quenched the flames on her flesh. The leaves dulled all her pain as euphoria kicked in. The bindweed vines so willful and unrelenting stretched into her window till they wrapped around her body and pulled her out of the fire.

The datura flowers bloomed over her body abnormally fast and died in a matter of seconds producing bright green thorny seed pods, more pods than should have been possible. They pierced her skin in multiple areas injecting their venomous poison deep within replacing her blood loss. The slit on her throat slowly began to close and her pale white skin now carried a hue of bluish-green.

The nettles wrapped around her flesh. Instead of stinging, they twisted and formed a thin gossamer garb to clothe her in their leaves and heal her burns.

She slumbered there for weeks neither waking to eat or drink till one night, under the shadow of the dark moon, her black eyes opened and the deep scream that escaped her mouth echoed through the swamp to the village so shrill, so unearthly, even the church bells went silent.

Oliviana sat up feeling slightly confused. *What had happened?* She looked around at her home. Half was burned down along with her books, her plants, and her jars of poisons. She picked brown spikes out of her skin giving no attention that she couldn't feel them anymore.

Something was different. She held her breath for several moments, then several moments more. The need to inhale never came. Her toes glided across the floor to the burnt wood that once was once her mantle. She blinked her black eyes and felt something new, something dark, something poisonous. She glided around the cinders of her once beloved home searching for the presence, but no matter where she looked, it seemed to be just out of reach.

She stopped and looked down at her own hands and finally saw what it was. Her. Her toes weren't touching the ground. Her fingers were blackened from knuckles to nails. And her once plain work clothes seemed to resemble something between a dress and liquid shadows.

"*Am I dead?*" Oliviana thought to herself. "Not dead, not alive, but something… in between," she heard whispers from within herself and felt the poison rush through her veins. The ghosts of the swamp and the poisons of the forest had come together and brought her back from the gates of death.

She exited what was left of her front door into the shadowy night and shouted, "spirits of my wood, speak! What has become of me?" The wind rushed through the trees and what was left of her scorched garden. She felt the voices not from around her, but within.

"We, We, We are with you. We, We, We who have been your ally. We, We, We who have brought death at your hands. We, We, We have come in your moment of need. We, We, We have made your blood poison, your skin the flesh of our fruit, and your soul has been fused with the spirit of usssssss…" the poisons within her whispered.

Oliviana should have been ash, but instead, here she was, not alive, not dead, but somewhere in the middle… and there she stayed for quite some time. Not scared, only uncertain. She couldn't see past the darkness that surrounded her once safe haven and refuge. She couldn't quite remember what was on the other side. How had she died? Who was it that killed her? It was all just… blank.

Time passed as if it meant nothing to her. Moments were weeks. Hours were months. The forest reclaimed half her burned-down home while the swamp reclaimed the other. A black sludge crept up the side of the structure from the bog below while belladonna, datura, and bindweed branches and vines completely covered the charred walls and corners of the homestead.

She existed floating somewhere between life and death, between time and space in the shadows for so long that she stopped speaking with only the poison running through her veins to keep her company… until one day, that changed.

"Please, help!" At first, the sounds meant nothing to her. Just some faint words echoing off the trees. "Someone, please!" She heard it again, the sounds of a child, a young boy, and for the first time in ages, she stirred.

The young boy stumbled out of the woods into the opening in front of her blackened refuge and stopped, eyes wide. Slowly, his desperation inched him forward, "Hello," he asked tentatively. She peered out of the shadows from inside her home now collapsing in on the burnt end.

The boy had welts from the stinging nettle all over his arms and legs and she could see he'd been crying. She moved forward further and he noticed movement inside. "Hello? I'm lost. Can you help me?" The boy cried.

She willed the door slowly open, "Come in," echoed from inside. He slowly inched his way forward crossing the threshold where it instantly felt cooler. She stood still in the shadows where the boy couldn't quite make her out. She tore a bit of the nettle fibers from skirts and a hand shot out of the darkness holding the scraps of fabric with her sallow skin and blacked fingers tips.

"Take these and bind your arms and legs. It will cut the sting and cool the rash," she told him matter-of-factly.

He hesitantly took the cloth and breathed a sigh of relief as the burning sensation dissipated. "Thank you," the boy said. "What is this?"

"The nettles." She replied, "the leaves will soothe the stalk that stings. Blessing and bane grow on the same stalk, you know. What can harm can also heal."

He collapsed onto the floor in relief. She glided forward and her voice echoed ever so slightly as she spoke, "how did you come to my hidden swamp in the woods?"

"I escaped", he replied. "I come from the nearby kingdom. After our wicked queen was assassinated, we celebrated for days. In all the commotion, many children in our village were kidnapped and put in the workhouse. This lady promised us sweets and a warm bed, but once she had us, she locked us in her basement selling us off for the highest coin. I escaped after she sold me to one of the queen's old guards. There's no ruler now and the kingdom has fallen into lawlessness. She sold another little boy to the guard weeks ago but no one's seen him since. Our carriage was ambushed by thieves and I ran." He concluded his tale in so few breaths, he had to heave upon finishing.

The poisoned queen, she thought. This was her doing. In her haste to end her reign, she hadn't thought about the after-effects. "Who is this woman who stole you and these other children?" She asked.

"I don't know her name," he replied.

"If I can help, would you take me to the place of this captress?"

The boy thought about what she asked for a few moments and bravely nodded.

They packed a few items for the journey, her throwing knives, some dried meat and cheese for the boy, her staff, and her charred black book of recipes and poisons. They then left her crumbling abode and followed the overgrown path out of the dark woods.

By nightfall, they'd reached the edge of the forest line and made their way in the shadows through back allies towards the workhouse. All the while, the boy tried not to notice that the feet of the woman in black never touched the ground.

"There it is," said the boy from the ally adjacent to his former prison. "What will you do?"

"Leave that to me," said Oliviana as she glided into the shadows and felt their darkness. She knew intrinsically from her recent predicament that somewhere between life and death was the world of light and dark. All she had to do was reach out to the shade and become one with the shadows.

The boy's eyes widened as he saw her figure slip into the darkness just outside the lamplight. He watched as the shadow stretched across the street and slipped inside the workhouse. Oliviana took in the disheveled nature of the sorrowful room. It stank of rotten food and unwashed bodies. As she glided down the hallway in the back, she heard a child's cry come from behind a door. At first, she tried the handle but it was locked. That was no matter to her.

She joined the shadows and slipped under the door to descend into the basement. The sight of cowering children in cages met her and her rage built. "Ahhh! Please stop", cried the little girl's voice. She waved her staff and shadows shot out in different directions towards the basement door and cages. One by one, they all unlatched and in an eerie echoing sound, she whispered, "go." And they all ran up the stairs to escape.

 She followed the sound further in till she found an anti-chamber. She slipped into the shadows and slid through the locked keyhole.

"Where is it?!" shouted the pinched woman as she reared back the whip in her hand and it cracked forward as the bound young girl in front of her covered in blood and dirty rags screamed out in pain.

Oliviana's shadow spread across the room and the woman shouted again, "Where's the list?!" As she lifted the whip a second time, Oliviana emerged from the darkness and grabbed it. The woman jumped back in shock. The cloth of Oliviana's sleeve lashed the woman across the face and neck as she grabbed the whip from her bony hands leaving a red angry nettle sting on her cheek.

She gasped and looked at the woman cloaked in black backing into a corner shaking. "But... but... I killed you," she said aloud. That's when Oliviana saw her face in the full light. Memories came flooding back, images of the doctor she had poisoned with his own mercury, his angry wife who had broken into her home, and her sneering smile as she left Oliviana bleeding out to burn.

Only one word escaped her lips, "go," and a shadow shot from her staff to the door latch as it blasted open and the young beaten girl ran. Oliviana looked back at the doctor's wife who was no longer sneering. "How?," the cornered woman asked aloud.

Oliviana glided towards her. "I've always lived in the darkness," she replied as she came closer and closer, "now... the darkness lives in me." The words came out in the softest whisper that echoed in the pinched woman's ear. She tried to get up but with a single wag of Oliviana's blacked finger she sat back and the mortar between the stone walls began to crack.

Bindweed sprouted from between the stones and began to weave around the sniveling woman. At first, she tried to break away, but very quickly they twisted and wrapped around her wrists and ankles. She sat there, bound, trying to scream but a "shhh" from beneath Oliviana's hood silenced her.

"I want to thank you for showing me the darkness within," she glided closer. "And now, I'd like to return the favor." She pulled one of her throwing knives out from her waist bag. "You see, I no longer need my precious herbs and berries. Because of you… I. Am. Poison." She pricked her left pointer finger as a drop of midnight black liquid oozed out.

With one touch to the bound woman's lips, the poison spread. Greenish-blue veins expanded out and the woman's eyes rolled back into her head. Roots split open the skin between her fingers and toes digging into the ground. Her hair fell out and her body began to twist into long lean stems. Big green shield-like leaves rolled out. White leathery flowers burst from her chest and wilted growing spiky pods that went from green to brown as they split open and burst with little seeds. The seeds fell and started their cycle up again.

Oliviana glided out of the underground anti-chamber once the cursed plant has finally stopped its cycle. It now covered the entire corner of the room. She left the empty workhouse to see all the children waiting outside. The boy ran up to her "Thank you! Thank you!" The kids all echoed his sentiment.

The young girl the doctor's wife had been whipping approached her. "Can you help me?" Tears stained her reddened dirty face as she lifted shaking fingers to hand Oliviana a small booklet. *This must be the list her captress was after,* she thought to herself. She opened it to see lists of names, amounts of money, family houses, and locations next to them. "She sold my sister to a nobleman. Can you help me find her?" The little girl asked her question with hope building in her eyes.

Oliviana looked down at the book of names in her hand realizing that each name was a child sold. She couldn't help but feel responsible. She had poisoned the woman's charlatan doctor husband. She had assassinated the wicked queen who at least punished the criminals of this now lawless kingdom.

"Yes," she said. "Yes. I will find your sister." She looked down at the names again. There were so many. Then and there she vowed to find every single name on that list if it was the last thing she ever did.

An idea began to form and she led the children through back alleys and side street shadows till she came to the now abandoned castle by the cliffs. With a flick of her staff, the shadows brought down the mote bridge and they swiftly made their way onto the castle grounds. There was dried meat in the kitchens and warm beds fit for royalty. Until this day, the wicked queen's reputation has been so fearsome, no one had dared to enter since her death.

Oliviana tended to each of their needs finding them rooms and necessities. To anyone else, she would have been a thing of nightmares, but for the children, she was their savior. With one touch, one kiss, she had learned she could sting, poison, and kill, but the children taught her that the same poison could numb pain, heal inflammation, and grant deep sleep. It all depended on how she used her new gifts. Her own words came back to her, "blessing and bane grow on the same stalk, you know. What can harm can also heal."

With the children settled, she made her way to the tower. The royal bedchamber stood empty as she glided around the large room. Having only been there once before, she made herself comfortable in her new home and as the sun rose, for the first time since she awoke from the land of death, she slept.

The following evening, after tending to the children, she took the booklet of names and houses and decided it was time to make some visitations. Over the following week, rumors of noble houses being abandoned spread with nothing left behind but bushels of thorn apple randomly sprouting in unusual places.

Each night, Oliviana ventured out with her staff and list of names. In the shadows, she visited knights, sheriffs, pubs, madams, pimps, and even clergy, always leaving behind her telltale poisonous beauties at every threshold she crossed.

The number of children in the castle ebbed and flowed. Some found their families. Others had none to return to. The returned ones told stories of the Lady in Black who never showed her face. They told tales of a dress that stings and heals, of shadows that opened doors, and of evil people who turned into flowers. Some believed she was a witch, others believed she was just another children's fairytale.

The villagers who hadn't seen lights in the castle for months were surprised to see smoke coming from the chimneys and candlelight shining down from the tower in the night sky. Glimpses of a black-clad woman were seen occasionally from the townsfolk below and accompanied

by the children's stories, the villagers began to leave
offerings at the castle bridge thankful to have their babes
safe at home again.

"Our Mother in Black" they called her, the Savior in the
Shadows, and on nights when those most desperate
needed her, they lit a black candle in the window and
prayed.

Mother in Black. I call your name.
Hear my plea through shadow by flame
To punish the wicked your name I enlist
Aide me now in this curse I twist

Oliviana listened to
the prayers brought to
her tower by wind and
shadow. Prayers to
save, to avenge, to
kill… she heard them
all.

And one by one…
she answered.

Author's note: The term "Black Magic" has a very sorted past within the occult. Historically, this concept stems from the word "Nigromancy" in the later Middle Ages from the Latin word for "black". It then later became synonymous with a similar word "Necromancy" which stems from the Latin word for "death" and was heavily associated with accusations during many witch trials. In the United States, the concept evolved further to draw racial implications by calling the folk practices of enslaved people of color "Black magic".

This verbiage has been used more by those outside the magical arts than within and in my opinion, it is a misnomer that I believe has no place in modernity. More importantly, there is no such thing as white magic or black magic. There is only magic and the desire of the practitioner directing it.

In this story, the archetype of a figure shrouded in black is not referring to themes of negativity or bane, but instead the shadow self. The self that feels and feeds the anger, the grief, the rage of revenge, and the closeness of death. Not only that, she represents the processing of those feelings. Finding peace in the shadows and the blessings of embracing your darkness. It's important not to assume that this figure and story are just meant to teach "black magic." That would be a grave misapprehension.

*For more on the origin of this story, reference the final section in par I, Cunning Tales.

9. Open Roads

Mercurial lived in a midsized cottage alongside a single dirt road. They met passersby who would stop for a bite to eat or sometimes the comfort of an extra bed for a weary traveler. Mercurial never turned down a kind stranger.

After many years of listening to those that had come and gone, yet never having traveled themselves, they sat by the fire tossing dandelion heads into the cinders from an old bouquet wishing one day for an opportunity to see the world. There was a crack of thunder and the sky outside lit up with a bolt of lightning. Mercurial set up startled from their fire gazing.

There was a knock at the door and they got up to see what the night had brought them. There stood a quaint, middle-aged woman in a red cloak with a hood that mostly obscured her face. "What a dreadful storm, dearie. Might you have an extra cot or bed for a traveler caught in the rain?" asked the scarlet-clad woman.

"Why, of course. Please come in. Come warm up by the fire." Mercurial replied.

They both made their way to the hearth welcoming the warmth. After settling down in two over-stuffed chairs, the woman heaved a sigh of relief. "I hope I didn't interrupt some important endeavor showing up at your doorstep," the woman said aloud.

"Oh no, you didn't interrupt anything at all", Mercurial said brushing aside their short curly hair. "I was just daydreaming. That's all I ever seem to do these days. I lived here my whole life but always dreamed of venturing out. It never seems to be the right time or something comes up and I end up putting it off for some future day."

"Well, maybe I can help with that. I'm Belinda, a simple weaver, at your service", said the woman as she stood and gave a slight bow.

"I'm Mercurial. It's lovely to meet you."

Belinda bent over to pull a small bag from beneath her scarlet cloak and pulled out a few items. First a hand mirror covered in knots of red thread. "No, not that," she said. "By the Old Ones, where is that thing?" Then she pulled out a small worn book with a red-stained cover. "Ahh, there it is. Let's see here. You say you want to travel, eh?"

"I… I don't really know. I know there's more out there for me I'm just not sure what. I feel stuck. I can't spend my eternity listening to the adventurous lives of others,"

Mercurial said with a sigh. They sat more upright as the woman across from them flipped through the book more feverishly. They could see scratched writing in dark red ink and lots of weird tiny symbols.

Finally, Belinda stopped, "I might have just the thing for you. Please let me repay you for allowing me refuge in such a dreadful storm." Outside, a loud crack of thunder came rolling through the landscape.

"Wha.. what is that?" Mercurial asked intrepidly.

"This?" she held up the dark red book, "oh, just a recipe book… of sorts, and I have here a recipe here just for you."

"A recipe? For what?" They asked confused.

"To open roads, my dearie. You wish for opportunities and I have just the thing," she said pointing to the page in her book. "But not today. This recipe is for tomorrow. Yes, it's perfect for a Wednesday morning."

They let the fire burn out and Mercurial made a nice cozy bed for Belinda. As they slept, Mercurial had a wild dream of red knots, dandelions, and places they'd never seen before. They awoke with the sun and a feeling of excitement.

They entered the main living space and immediately smelled the delicious aroma of bacon and fried eggs. Belinda was cooking up a bountiful breakfast. "I hope you don't mind, dear. I just couldn't help myself. I hope you woke up hungry," Belinda said. Mercurial couldn't remember the last time someone had cooked for them. It was quite an unexpected treat.

Once their meal was done and their bellies were full, Mercurial asked, "Was this the recipe from your book? I appreciate the kindness but I'm afraid nothing has changed".

"On no. This was just because I enjoy the smell of bacon in the morning, and travelers need their sustenance. But now that you bring it up, let's have ourselves a little chat, shall we?" Belinda beckoned them over to the hearth where she took out her red book. "Tell me, dear, now what were you doing right before I arrived yesterday? Think."

"Yesterday?" they said. "Oh, well I was just sitting here by the fire…"

"Yes, and what else? Be specific."

"Well, I was sitting here tossing dried-out dandelions from an old bouquet there". They pointed to the remaining dried yellow flowers left on the mantle.

"And" coaxed Belinda.

"And just wishing I had more opportunities to see the world and experience more of life than just this old roadside cottage."

"That's what I thought I heard", Belinda said to herself amused. Mercurial quizzically sat up about to ask what she meant by that but Belinda spoke first. "Well you called and so I have answered." She pulled her small book out from beneath her sleeve and continued, "you were so close, I just couldn't help myself." Belinda smiled knowingly, "you want to open roads to new opportunities and that's exactly what I've come to offer you".

"To offer me?" Mercurial asked curiously. "I thought you said you were a weaver. How can a weaver offer me such an ask?"

"Oh my dear, I should have been more clear. While I am a weaver, sometimes I weave thread and fabric, and other times I find myself weaving a little magic. You seem to have all the garments you need, so how about I repay your hospitality with a charm?"

Mercurial sat there for a moment slightly stunned. They had wished for opportunities and opportunities came knocking. What were they to do? Refuse? She seemed like such a kind lady. What harm could there be? "Why not?" They said finally. "I could use a little more luck in my life."

"Oh, this isn't luck, my dear. This is magic."

"Do you see this symbol here?" Belinda continued, "this is the symbol of your namesake. Did you know you are

named after a great god?
A god that certainly
knew how to go places
and carry very important
messages. Some called
him Hermes but others
called him Mercury. He
was quite the queer one.
He had the gift of flight
and the honor of
ascending to the heavens
or descending into the
depths of the

underworld. And did you know… he absolutely loves
dandelions." She watched Mercurial's face as they took in
what she said.

They looked at Belinda and then down at the glyph
scribbled in red ink on the page. It was a funny sort of box
with 4 circles and Xs. They thought for a few moments
taking everything in. They let out a loaded breath and
asked, "What do we do with it?"

"Oh isn't that the question, dearie," Belinda replied
knowing she'd piqued their interest. "Nothing comes
without sacrifice I'm afraid." She got out a blank page
from the back of her book and copied the symbol on it.
"May I see your right hand, dear?"

Mercurial held out their hand and before they knew it,
Belinda had pricked their little finger with the clasp that
fastened her red cloak now draped over the back of the
chair. "Ouch!"

"As I said, a small sacrifice for new opportunities."

She took Mercurial's pinky finger now sporting a ruby droplet at the tip and pressed it into the symbol on the paper. "It's a beautiful Wednesday morning," she said almost as if simply making conversation. "Did you know Wednesday is dedicated to your namesake? Not only is it the day of Mercury it's also smack dab in the middle of the week. Three days before and three days after. It's almost as if today is the day we can get a clear view of all other days, other roads, other… opportunities," she finished as she gathered the remaining dandelions.

From Mercurial's viewpoint, several things seemed to happen very quickly. As Belinda stood near the mantle, she splashed a sprinkle of liquid from a small bottle in her palms that seemed to come from nowhere. The reddish liquid hit the dying embers in the fireplace and with a sizzle, the flames exploded upwards ablaze with a crackling fury.

Belinda looked up at Mercurial with a side smile. "Who doesn't love a flame stoked by magic?" she asked with a sly wink.

"Now take these," she continued as she handed them the dandelions. "toss them into the flames," and they did just that. "Now take this," she handed them the small paper with their blood stamped on the symbol. "Hold it between your palms at hearts your center and say this command eight times from the depths of your soul:"

Mercury, Old One, Divine Androgyne
Open all roads
Open all doors
Open all pathways of communication
May all signs be clear
May all paths to
Advantage and abundance
Be unblocked
By your seal;
By your name
I evoke your power

"Upon the final word, deliver the charged seal in your palms to the flame," Belinda finished. All the hairs on the back of Mercurial's neck stood on end. The words were simple but held a command in them that sent a shiver of excitement down their spine.

Mercurial repeated the words eight times and a deep richness in their throat rang out. It was as if a cacophony of melodic voices from the depths of their soul joined them in song. The words escaped their lips like ribbons of magic and the dandelions disintegrated into ash that floated up the chimney and upon the final word, they tossed the paper symbol into the fire.

Sparks burst and the flames shot up with licks of purple and silver joining the now-red smoke gliding up the chimney. "I think it's time to step outside, dearie," Belinda said. They walked toward the door and exited. Mercurial looked up to see the red smoke like a beacon in the dawn light. They backed up to get a better view when Belinda interrupted with a clearing of her throat. Her eyes met

Mercurials and looked down. They followed her gaze to see where they stood.

The single road that had always been there was now wider and Mercurial realized they weren't standing in one road but the center cross-section of eight different roads all leading out in different directions. "Open roads," they said aloud as they met Belinda's beguiling smile.

"It looks like you have some options, my dear," she said. "The roads have been opened for you and each one will take you on a new adventure. One of advantage and new opportunities."

"What about my cottage," Mercurial asked.

"I'll stay here and watch over your home for you. I do just love meeting new travelers. Perhaps I'll meet someone else who could use some of my guidance," she said.

"And if you ever find yourself homesick, who knows? Perhaps I'll just bring your cottage to you," were her final words followed by a laugh as she walked back into the cottage leaving Mercurial standing in the center of an eight-way crossroads. They turned to thank her, but upon looking back, they saw Belinda was gone along with the little house. There was nothing left but a puff of red chimney smoke and the faint sound of an echoing cackle.

"There's no turning back now," Mercurial said aloud taking one step forward, and with a hopeful smile, walked towards the rising sun.

10. For the Love of Myrtle

There once was a sacred tree that stoically resided in a
southern city center. It was known by the local villagers as
the Crepe tree. It was so clean and pure, its flowers so
white and its trunk so grey and smooth. No matter the
heat of the summer, it would bloom, and its beauty would
make even the most sweltering stop to admire it.

One night, in the hot evening air of August, the tree full of
ruffled white blooms was swaying in the breeze when it
heard a beautiful song wafting in the wind.

> *My long lost lover*
> *Come and find me*
> *My sweet soulmate*
> *Come to set me free*

The voice was sweet but sad with such a longing. The tree leaned forward to hear more.

My companion for life
I long to know you
My partner my love
With a heart so true

The ivory flowers bloomed brighter and brighter slowly turning from a crisp white to a pale pink. Something had awoken within the tree. Something new. *"I must know this voice."* Thought the tree as it cast out its branches further into the sky to listen.

I call out to the winds
To bring me true love
Make their way to me
By the heavens above

The tree standing tall swayed in the wind, soaking up the wistful notes, turning its light pink petals to a now fiery fuchsia. The heat rose and the local villagers gathered as their sacred stoic white tree of purity was now alive, a fiery bright pink. They wiped the sweat beading on their brows as the heat of the night was cooled only by the breeze carrying the sweet song.

By all that is
And by all that will be
Bring my long lost love
To me

The tree stretched taller than ever before, its branches sticking straight out reaching for the melodic notes in the air. The crowd gathering watched in wonder as the fuchsia blooms deepened to a scarlet red as if its limbs were cut open bleeding soft plumes of ruffled petals.

The villagers could see the waves of heat now emanating from their sacred tree once so cool, pure, and white, the branches now erect, glistening like rubies in the moonlight. The singer came forward and the townspeople parted as they strode nearer singing their song.

The tree no longer able to be still started to quiver and the crimson flowers began to spark. The crowd stood back as flames burst from the tree, branches covered in small explosions of fire.

Mesmerized, they all watched and the singer was drawn forward unafraid of the burning tree. The flames died down and the singer approached the giant pile of ash. The smoke cleared and a gasp rang out. There in the pile of dying cinders stood a figure, a human figure.

The magic of the song had ignited something deep with the sacred Crepe tree. Something its soul had never known… it's mate. The singer's song carried by the winds blew the ash away and they came together and embraced. "Your sweet melody has ignited a passion within me," said the figure. "What do I call you, my love?"

"Myrtle, my name is Myrtle", the singer replied. The beautiful name spoken was the final note to their love song.

The villagers watched as the two wrapped arm-in-arm and
began to walk away from the once revered home of the
tree in the southern city center. As they did, buds sprouted
in the wake of their footsteps swiftly growing into smaller
versions of the tree. Only now, as they bloomed, the
flowers emerged in colors of pink, fuchsia, lavender, violet,
red, and of course, white.

The townsfolk told the story of this miracle for years to
come. They told their children and their children's children
till it was only thought of as a fabled tale. But to this day,
the trees they now call the loving Crepe Myrtle, line the
streets, yards, and forests of the land.

And on the hottest nights, when the only relief is a cool
evening breeze, you might hear the sweet song in the wind
that created this miraculous monument to love.

My long lost lover
Come and find me
My sweet soulmate
Come to set me free

My companion for life
I long to know you
My partner my love
With a heart so true

I call out to the winds
To bring me true love
Make their way to me
By the heavens above

Author's note: Growing up in Texas, the Crepe Myrtle tree has been ever-present in my life. It's one of the most common trees in the south because it thrives in our climate. It blooms in early summer with ruffles of white, lavender, pink, and red. As the summer gets hotter, the grass turns brown, and many plants suffer from heat and drought, but the Crepe Myrtle thrives. In August, when the triple-digit temperatures soar, it blooms its brightest. The fuchsia flowers pepper the houses, streets, neighborhoods, cities, and landscapes. Sometimes, during long summers, it's the only colorful hue left when water is scarce. When the petals finally begin to fall and the seed pods grow, we know that relief is just around the corner. As the pods turn brown and split open into 6 equal sections creating a star, it carries with it magic in the shape of the 6-ways: the cardinal directions north, east, south, west as well as the Above, and Below. When they split, we feel the changing of the seasons, the night grows longer, and the winter holidays are on their way. In the spring, the new little green buds push off the old brown husks and the cycle begins anew. This ever-present tree in my life has been a constant guide for my wheel of the year and has always inspired in me a deep love for its splendor. This story taps into that love and the very nature of a tree that can bring us such beauty, such grace, in a time of even the most inhospitable heat. I hope the love of the Crepe Myrtle warms your heart as much as it does mine.

11. Witch Bottles

It had been years since she had lost her beloved Gran. The town Una lived just outside of had slowly rebuilt over the last two decades and while not quite thriving, it was attracting more and more villagers.

No one was left from the original township after the incident that took place 20-some-odd years ago after she lost her gran and learned of her heritage. When people came to the empty homes and central meeting house, they assumed that it was deserted due to a brush fire or a long past plague and began to rebuild. Folks had noticed her little cottage farm up the hillside and even brought her neighborly tidings.

Some began to visit her for aid in the early days. With her herb garden and knowledge of the land, she had become somewhat of a local wise woman to the townsfolk over the years, and none were the wiser of her past.

One day there was a knock at her door and when she answered, there stood a middle-aged person with short shaggy hair, freckles, and a friendly smile. "Can I help you?" Una asked.

"I hope so. I've journeyed very far and found myself having an accident in your woods back there," they said holding up their hand with a large blistering burn. "A little bird told me you might be able to help."

"Oh dear! Please come inside. I'll fetch fresh water and some aloe from the garden," Una said quickly. "Sit here. I'll be right back", and she was swiftly out the door.

The person sat there at the kitchen table hand outstretched until Una returned. She washed the wound and smeared a heaping amount of thick clear jelly atop the burn. It is cooling relief was visible on the person's face and they let out a breath, "Thank you so much. That feels so much better."

"Happy to help," she said. "I'm Una. Who do I have the pleasure of inviting into my home?"

"My apologies, ma'am. I'm Mercurial," they replied and stuck out their hand without injury. Una took it in hers and smiled feeling their warmth.

"It's lovely to meet you, Mercurial. You said you've journeyed far? Tell me about your travels."

Mercurial told her a fantastic tale of their disappearing house and the life they left behind years ago. They told her of the time they broke their ankle in a cliffside village and three sisters healed them with word and touch alone. They told her of a town where criminals and the cruel gentry disappeared leaving behind gardens of beautiful but deadly flowers. They told her of seeing a magical tree that made people fall in love and even a story of the little yellow bird who told them where to go after they burnt their hand on this morning's breakfast.

"I'm sure that sounds like a fantasy, but it's all true. I wouldn't have believed it myself if I hadn't seen it," Mercurial said. "I remember the day I left home hoping for new opportunities, I never would have expected what was to come."

"I believe you," Una said with a slightly cocked head and a smirk.

She invited Mercurial to stay at her home till their hand was healed and over the next few weeks, they began to form a close kinship. Weeks turned into months and months turned into a whole year. Their bond grew into a love Una had never expected. Mercurial became her everything and she was theirs.

Unfortunately, the gossip of the villagers began to grow and that was something that brought Una great fear. She still remembered that day over 20 years ago when the old townsfolk came for her and her Gran. Lady Delusor was the loudest gossip and she was a mean woman who had always hated Una. She spread ugly words about the "unholy coupling" of Una and her companion and whipped up the villagers into a frenzy.

"Who is she?"
"Is he her lover?"
"Thank goodness they live outside of town. I'd hate to have that shoved in my face every day," the gossipers would say.

Mercurial tried to comfort Una but they didn't know the fullness of Una's past. One day, there was a knock at their door and Una went to answer followed by Mercurial in support. They opened the entryway and there stood Lady Delusor, a basket of fresh sweet bread in her hands.

"Hello, lad... I mean both of you," Lady Delusor said catching herself, not knowing exactly how to address both of them.

"Good morning, Lady Delusor," said Mercurial as Una nodded her head in the Lady's direction. While she was a few years younger than Una, she looked and acted much older.

"How can we help you, ma'am?"

"Well, I've come to offer you this sweet bread for all you've done for the community over the years," the Lady replied.

"Why, thank...", Una said but was cut off by the Lady continuing.

"But your help won't be necessary anymore." She looked them both up and down in the doorway and her smile began to crack. "We don't approve of this 'situation' going on up here, us in the town I mean. I wanted you to know we won't be coming to you anymore and we'd prefer to not see the likes of you down in the square. It's unnatural and frankly confusing to the children who've always seen you as kind. Now they don't know what to think and we have to set them straight."

She finished her proclamation and stood there with a satisfied thin smile on her lips. Angrily, Mercurial stepped forward and said in a stern but controlled voice, "You came all the way up here to tell us to fuck off with sweet bread?"

The Lady Delusor blanched at the cursing, recovered, and held her head high. "It's common courtesy to deliver harsh news with something to soften the blow."

Una stood there in frozen silence. She was paralyzed by her memory of the town turning against her. Mercurial took the basket and tossed it behind them scattering the loaves to the corner of the kitchen. "What a kindness," they said dripping in sarcasm.

"Good day," Lady Delusor said with a slight nod and a cooked grin. She turned and left with a maddening confidence. Una stood there frozen in fear while Mercurial wrapped their arms around her shivering frame.

"It's ok. She's gone, now," they reassured her.

"You don't understand," Una broke down. "They've done this before. The townsfolk turned on us when I was young." Una had told Mercurial about what happened two decades ago but had not told her the final part. The part where she called up the monstrous fairies and creatures of the forest in revenge. They didn't know just how much power she held and hoped to never call up again.

A few days went by and when nothing happened, Una began to breathe a bit more easily. But after the third day, Mercurial began to feel sick. A fever broke out in them that seemed to only grow each day. They wouldn't eat or drink anything more than sips of water and a bit of broth.

Una used all her knowledge of herbal medicine to no avail until a thought occurred to her. What if this wasn't natural? What if this was... something else? She took her old chicken bones to the fireplace and said the charm while shaking them in her palms.

Bones of my land
Only truth do tell me
If ye fall vertical
A yes my answer be
If the answer be no
On the horizon do fall
Spirits of my land
Your knowledge I do call

"Is the illness that befalls my love Mercurial naturally born?" She asked aloud. She cast them in the flickering lights of the hearth and all three bones fell horizontally. "Oh no," she said to herself. "Is the illness born from a baneful intention?" The bones fell in a neat row all three pointing up and down dictating an affirmative answer.

"How could a hex make its way into this house?" she thought to herself. She had always thought herself to be the only witch in the town. *Who else would know the arts as she did? How did someone slip past her woodland protectors?*

She knew it was time to act fast. She moved the old stone that hid her Gran's grimoire by the mantle and feverishly flipped through. There was a pair of pages she had seen long ago but never felt the need to use their instructions. She found the section and gazed upon the drawing of bottles. There were two different workings, one on each page. Both looked similar but carried different instructions.

The first was said to force a witch to remove a curse, while the second page stated that the bottle was to protect one from future malevolence. She went back to the first page and read more fully:

To Return a Curse:
Fill a glass bottle with:
-sharp pins/ needles/ iron nails
-urine of the afflicted person

Place at the hearth by a blazing fire and wait for the urine to boil. The witch who cast the curse will begin to feel the pain of a full bladder forcing them to remove the curse. Should the bottle shatter in the heat, the witch who cast the curse will experience a complete rebound of their working back upon themselves.

"Sounds like a win/win," she said aloud to herself and decisively grabbed an old wine bottle from a shelf and some pins and needles from her mending kit. She slipped into Mercurial's room and took her bedpan back to the hearth. She placed the pins inside and filled the rest of the bottle with her love's urine. She sealed it with the cork and held it up to see her handiwork.

Knowing the witch might confront her should she continue, she bravely placed the bottle by the fire and added kindling till it was hot and bright. After a few minutes, little bubbles began to form at the bottom and the pins began to dance in the golden boiling liquid.

Thirty minutes went by and after no knock at her door from any witch, the boiling bottle showed the first signs of a crack followed by another and another. The glass suddenly burst, spilling the hot steaming liquid, and putting out half the fire with a hiss. It sizzled and sour smoke poured up the flue. "Well, it's done now," she said aloud and for the first time in days, she heard her love's faint voice calling for her.

As she went to comfort them, the putrid smoke coalesced out her chimney in an unattractive dance swirling back into the village and right to the doorstep of one very unhappy lady.

Several days went by. Mercurial fully recovered and Una told them the truth of what she'd done. Together they made a second bottle, the one marked as protective from future malevolence. Which read as follows.

To Protect from Future Malevolence
Fill a glass bottle with:
-pins/ needles
-iron nails
-broken glass/ mirror.
May every household member place:
-fingernail & toenail clippings
-hair
-urine

Seal with a cork and wax to never again be opened. Bury on your land near your place of dwelling and all future malevolent curses, hexes, and workings will be trapped by your decoy bottle instead of making their way to you.

They buried the bottle together by the old oak at the side of the house and as they were washing up, a young boy from the village ran up the hill. "Una! Una! Come quick! We need your help", the boy said.

"What's happened?" Una asked with haste.

"The Lady! The Lady Delusor! She's gravely ill. Please come quick!"

Una took a moment and glanced over at Mercurial with a knowing look. *The witch who cast the curse will experience a complete rebound of their working back upon themselves* she recounted from the passage in her Gran's book. *The sweet bread* she remembered. They hadn't eaten it but they had begrudgingly accepted it into their home… well, Mercurial had and they had been the one to become afflicted by its malevolence.

"Let me get my things," she said and went inside to grab a bag, a few medicinal herbs, and the book. They made their way down to the home adjoining the meeting house, the house of Lady Delusor. The whispering villagers parted as she and Mercurial together glided up the walkway and into her home. They made their way to her bedside and she told everyone, "Leave us. The Lady and I have work to do." Everyone left but Mercurial, and the moment the door closed, Una gave it a glance as it locked of its own accord.

The Lady opened her eyes and when she took in the faces of Una and Mercurial, they widened and she tried to scream but quickly Una put a finger to her lips and no sound would escape the Lady's mouth.

"You paid my house a visit, Lady Delusor," Una said, her voice dripping in saccharin disdain. "It was some sweet bread I believe you brought, wasn't it?"

The Lady's eyes now wide with fear looked up at her.

"I've come to return the favor," she said as she sat down on the side of the bed. The Lady glared up at her with hatred in her eyes. "What's wrong? Cat got your tongue?" teased Una. "Go on, you may speak now."

"You deserve what you get, witch! I was there. I remember you're wickedness all those years ago," the Lady spat. Una was caught off guard. "I was just a child when you conjured the monsters of the forest and killed my parents. I hid in our cellar and when I emerged days later after the screaming had stopped, the town was covered in the blood your hands spilled. I tried to get help but a storm had washed the streets clean of your monstrous deeds."

Una sat there still in her silence. This was an unexpected turn of events. She was not proud of that day decades ago. She was still a girl herself locked in grief and survival. After the town had been massacred, she had called up a storm that flooded the village for days washing away the carnage. How had she not known there was a lone survivor?

Mercurial looked at Una questioningly.

She steeled herself, took a deep breath, and spoke. "I... I didn't have a choice. I was only a girl myself and your village murdered my Gran, coming for me only days later. I chose to survive," She looked over at Mercurial and her composure broke. With a deep sigh, she turned back to the sick woman laying in bed, tears began rolling down her eyes as she retold the most horrific day of her life. "I'm sorry," she said. "You should never have suffered for their sins, nor should you be punished for mine."

The Lady's stiff body began to relax and her face softened. She had waited over 20 years to reveal herself to the witch who murdered her family. She had put so much ire and hatred into kneading that bread to curse her lifelong enemy. She had never expected an actual apology or empathy. Something inside her broke as she saw not the person responsible for her family's death, but a once young grieving girl desperately trying to survive.

"I never begrudged you your companion," the Lady said. I just needed to build a case against you in the village. For that, I too am sorry." Tears began streaming down both their faces, the afternoon of revelations almost too large to all take in.

She pulled out her Grans book and a small bag of herbs. "Fetch me the kettle, my love," Una told Mercurial, and they did so. She poured hot water into a small cup and a few teaspoons of Nettles and Angelica root and stirred counterclockwise while whispering words from the book:

I untwist
I unbind
This curse
So entwined
Out of body
Out of mind
Malice begone
No more maligned

Una stirred and spoke the charm 13 times then offered a sip to Lady Delusor. She sat up weakly and sipped from the cup, the warm liquid slowly filling her throat and stomach. Moments later, she took her first deep breath without struggle and the color began to return to her cheeks. Her fever broke and tears of relief poured from the corners of her eyes. The curse was broken but not only that, the decades-old hate and anger were gone too.

They both looked into one another's eyes, years of hurt and trauma slowly beginning to heal. Una and Mercurial left the Lady's house with the thanks of the villagers. On the way home, Una told them the secret she had been keeping for all these years and they lovingly held her hand all the way back up the hill.

That night, they were sitting by the fire with Mercurial's head in her lap when Una spoke. "Maybe it's time to move on from here. Maybe I've spent enough time in this cage of preservation, walled in by my fear."

Mercurial looked up at her, "Where shall we go?" At just that moment a thunderous bolt of lightning struck outside and the wind began to howl. There was a knock at the front of the house and they both looked up.

Together they went to the entryway and opened the door. There was a slightly older woman standing there with a blood-red cloak and hood obscuring her face. "Hello, dearie. I thought we might one day meet again," Belinda said as she looked up at them with a glint in her eye and a crooked smile on her face. "Might I come in?"

Author's note: This tale is inspired by two old apotropaic rites known as witch bottles. These were bottles filled with urine, pins, and hair used by cunning folk or "witch doctors" for warding off or turning back malefic witchcraft.

12. The Seven Holy Siblings

There once were Seven Holy Siblings and the first was called Sunday. He was devoted to the Sun and worshiped at the Solar Temple. He was a strong powerful protector and had the gift of healing illnesses of the body. He always smiled bringing happiness to all who sought him. His dwelling was covered in sunflowers, marigolds, and dandelions.

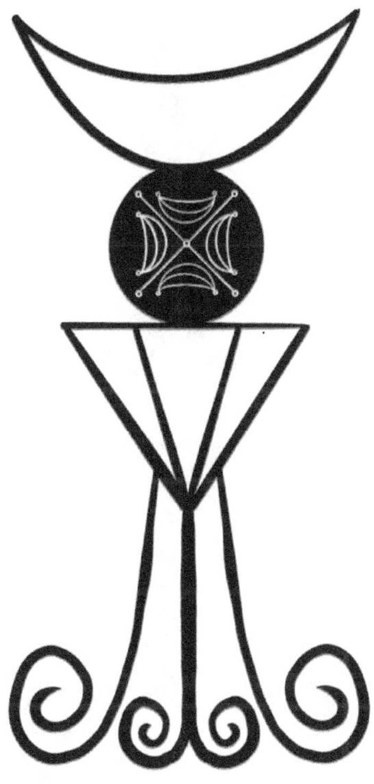

The second sibling was called Monday and she was devoted to the moon. She resided at Temple Luna by the sea adorned in moonflower. She was a water priestess and the keeper of dreams. She was known for her gifts of intuition, foresight, and empathy. She was a great Oracle and people came for miles to seek divinatory services, water, and moon magic.

The third sibling was called Tuesday and was devoted to Mars. He held court at the Martian Temple and Armory. He was a great and virile defender. His gifts of brute force and strength made him the champion of the people and he led armies in victorious battles. With him on your side, no challenge would be too great to be accomplished.

The fourth sibling was named Wednesday and they served the Temple of Mercury adorned by dandelions and lavender. They were the head organizer and messenger of the siblings having the gift of encouraging or calming discourse. They were a keeper of memories and thoughts and a great philosopher. They were a wonderful public speaker and people would travel to the Temple to seek guidance from Wednesday in matters of travel, business, and new opportunities.

The fifth sibling went by the name Thursday and was the head of the golden Temple of Jupiter. He was the most loyal sibling, a great leader and advisor in financial and legal matters. People came to him for gifts of wealth, prosperity, and improvements in familial and social standing. Supported by his sibling Mercury, he was known to aid in a thriving business and opportunities for success and gain.

The sixth sibling was named Friday and she was the most beautiful. She devoted herself to the Temple of Venus and kept a harem of lovers around her. She was a great poet and supporter of the arts. People came to her to find romance and aid them in marriage and fertility. She gladly bestowed gifts of beauty, love, and friendship to all those who sought her Venusian temple.

The seventh and final sibling was called Saturday. He stood guardian at the black Temple of Saturn and was known to be stoic and nocturnal. He was a great magician who trafficked with spirits and was known as the keeper of curses and bindings. Surrounded by nightshades and thorn trees, his temple only saw the bravest and most determined of visitors. They brought gifts of farm goods and once a year called upon him to bless their crops with sacrificial blood.

There once were Seven Holy Siblings and now you know them all: Sunday, Monday, Tuesday, Wednesday, Thursday, Friday, and Saturday. They stand sentinel of their temples and every seven days, each, in turn, reigns supreme, bringing you their presence and gifts all week long. All you have to do is ask.

Author's note: This isn't so much a story as much as a parable and teaches a method of personifying the days of the week and their connections to their corresponding planets. The magic is based loosely on The Three Books of Occult Philosophy by Henry Cornelius Agrippa, Book II, Chapter VVII: Of the tables of the planets, their virtues, forms, and what divine names, intelligences, and spirits are set over them. I was also inspired by Traditional Witchcraft, a Book of Cornish Ways by Gemma Gary which approaches planetary work from a folk magic perspective. This parable corresponds to the final grimoire in part III of this book, the Cunning Compendium, chapter 13. Talismans of the Seven Holy Siblings. It teaches how to create paper talismans using the knowledge woven in this story.

13. Death, Life, and Pine Cones

Years ago, Tessa met the Yellow Bird, and he helped her gain control of her life. After her mistress had passed, she had left Tessa everything, her home, her finances, her wardrobe, everything.

"A Lady leaving her house to her servant, my goodness! She must have been quite the companion."

"That's quite a rise of station."

"Her mistress must have truly cared for her."

The gossip ran from kindly to suspicious. None were the wiser that she had been the one to command it, her mistress always under her spell.

The Man in Yellow visited Tessa nightly and every morning the Bird flew out her window. Together, they had a daughter who was gifted with her mother's talents. Tessa introduced her little girl to the Yellow Bird and she instantly took a liking to him. He had opened the gates to other worlds, shared with her the secrets of the Old Ones, and she began to write everything down he taught her. Tessa wrote down how to bless a home, how to divine, how to attract and repel love, to heal the sick, to appease the woodland creatures, and even talk to the dead. She knew one day she'd want to pass down her knowledge.

Unfortunately, while Tessa could survive the gossip of her rise in station, she couldn't hide a fatherless child. The night they came to arrest her for fornication, the Yellow Bird told her of their soon-to-be arrival. She packed a few clothes, some provisions, and her book, and with her daughter in tow, snuck into the night moments before the magistrate's arrival.

For days, the bird led them west through woodsy terrain and eventually out the other side. She knew they wouldn't follow that far, not into the darkness of the forest.

Days turned to a week and they finally emerged out the other end to a large meadow beyond a hill above a small budding village. Tessa slowly built a quaint cottage under the shade of a giant old oak. It had a few rooms, a fireplace, and a practical kitchen all while beginning a healthy garden of wheat, herbs, and vegetables. She sewed seeds she found growing wild in the woods and whatever the yellow bird offered her. Sometimes he came with other creatures he called fair folk carrying sustenance and she would in return give them offerings of milk and whisky she distilled herself.

Her daughter grew into a fine maiden and soon men from the nearby town came to call on her. The villagers believed Tessa to be a widow which freed her and her daughter from any semblance of shunning and very quickly her daughter fell in love with the most handsome man in town and was married. She and her new husband moved down into town to a small cottage and for a while they were happy.

On a Sunday evening, Tessa gifted her daughter a large lemon stuck with 36 pins of various colors to bless their new home. With each pin, she said the cunning words her lover had taught her:

Blessings by the majestic sun
Good fortune by the lady moon
Aradian charm do I charge
Gifts of advantage so opportune

Her daughter's new husband was a bit wary and thought it a strange custom but was happy to have such a beauty for a wife and looked the other way.

A few years passed and try as they might, Tessa's daughter could not conceive a child. It began to create a rift between the couple and he began to resent her. It started with cruel things about her likeness to her mother, Tessa, and would even refer to her as that "ole' hag." He began to drink more and would sometimes get physically violent. She felt at a loss for what to do.

She confided to her mother, "He's become so unkind and says the most awful things when drunk. I think he's started seeking satisfaction elsewhere. What should I do? Can you help me?" she begged her. Tessa thought for a moment and decided to seek guidance from the Yellow Bird, her daughter's true father.

That night, she went into the woods and called out, "Yellow Bird, Man of the forest, I ask for your aid once more. How can I help our daughter conceive?" The bird flew down and the Man in Yellow landed before her. "Our daughter stems from our magical union. She is magic born and so shall her child be," he said to Tessa.

She realized his words were true and let out a sigh. "Can nothing be done?" she asked him.

"Of course, my dear, my sweet, my witch," he replied. "Now listen closely…"

Tessa invited her daughter to an afternoon visit. Tessa pulled out her book and together they cast a spell to bring back harmony to the home using skullcap, dandelion, and rose petals. Then she turned to where she had jotted down the spell the Yellow Bird had told her. "Before returning home, gather a fully ripened pine cone from the woods," she said. "Place it under your bed and say the following charm three times."

Babe of pine
Come into my home
Bring unto me
A Babe of my own

"Be sure it's the correct time of conception and goodness willing, you will soon be with child." Tessa finished instructing her daughter and together they picked the perfect plump pine cone at the forest's edge. She went home, placed it under her bed hidden next to a box with several bottles of herbs, pins, cloth, and her small diary of her mother's recipes, then said the cunning words three times.

That night her husband came home drunk from the tavern, something that had been happening more frequently in recent months. She disrobed him and washed his naked body. He was surprised but willingly accepted the attention. That night they made a baby and for a few months, there was peace.

Her mother Tessa visited regularly bringing herbs, tea, and hearty root vegetables from her garden. The villagers began to feel slightly uneasy with the small trinkets she would hang around their house: a horseshoe at the door, a bottle that several children saw her bury in their yard, a garland of garlic inside the front door.

"It's not right," they'd say.

"No godly woman traffics with such items."

"I wonder why he allows that in his home?"

The harmony began to dwindle as her belly grew and the father-to-be started coming home from the tavern drunk and incoherent. He listened to the gossip of the townsfolk in his stupor and began to believe that maybe there was something more to his wife and her mother.

Tessa's daughter awoke one morning in her third trimester to the splash of ale on her face. "What is this?" Her husband shouted holding the box of items from under their bed along with the pine cone. "WHAT IS THIS?!" he shouted again. "The neighbors keep telling me I married a heathen but I tell 'em 'No! She's a good one, my wife,' but then I find this!" He yells pointing at the box.

"This isn't natural," he said seething. "I allowed your mother's strange customs in the beginning but not anymore. Not in my house! This is the devil's work!" he shouted throwing the pine cone against the wall, smashing it to pieces.

Pain shot up her stomach and she screamed out in agony. Her husband stood back shocked for a moment till he put it all together: the cone under the bed, her belly ripe with child, her screams at the cone's destruction. "You coaxed a child into the world by witchery!?" he said with astonishment. He hadn't been sure till this moment and his righteous anger exploded.

He pulled her to her feet and in only her nightgown, he shoved her out the front door clutching her belly. "Begone, witch!" he shouted. "Take you and your devil child and never return or find yourself at the end of a noose!"

The villagers watching were in shock as they stood back speaking amongst themselves.

"Did he say, witch?"

"I knew she was a strange one! Her and her mother."

"Don't look child", a mother said covering her son's eyes. "Best not to risk her gaze."

So quickly they turned on her as her husband continued to push her further and further out of the village. She stumbled her way up the hill through the meadow of blooming daisies that led to her mother's house. "Mother!" she called out as she crawled to the door bleeding from below.

Tessa answered the door gasping as she picked her daughter up and carefully brought her to the back bedroom. She lay there in a cold sweat white as a sheet. Her breathing was labored and Tessa knew the baby was coming early.

She gathered an elixir of poppy for pain, linens, and hot water from the kettle and began the arduous task of helping her grandchild come into this world. It was bloody and violent. Screams rang out, the sheets were soaked in crimson, and before long, a small baby girl emerged. Tessa's daughter breathed deeply in relief, but the blood wouldn't stop coming.

Tessa handed her daughter the tiny baby girl and they both cried. She looked into her daughter's teary eyes knowing how this would end. The dying mother looked up from her newborn child to her mother and said, "Promise me you'll care for her. Promise me you'll shield her from this. Promise me you'll give her a normal life safe and free from magic."

"I promise, my child", Tessa sobbed. "I'll raise her as my very own."

The bleeding began to slow and a stillness washed over the air. "What will you name her, my daughter?", Tessa asked. And with a final breath, she said, "Una. Her name shall be Una."

 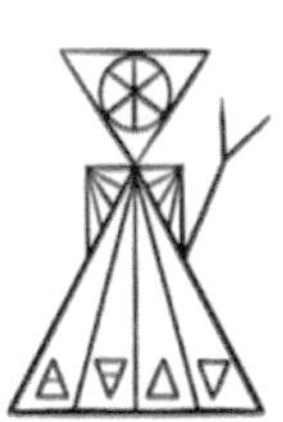 

Epilogue

Tessa, now a grandmother, had just put Una to bed when
she began sewing up the mouth of a taglocked paper doll.
The Man in Yellow had gifted her knowledge of poppet
magic and this particular charm would seal the loose lips of
one who might have too much to say. She placed a candle
over it and said the words necessary many times over:

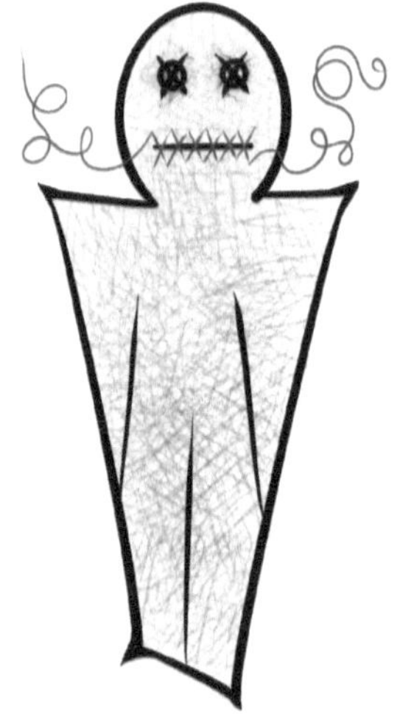

Spirits of old
Aid me this hour
Silencing spirit forces
Lend me your power
Bound paper doll
In image of thee
My will be done
So shall it be

She tucked her book of magic
behind a loose stone by the
mantle and she, along with
the Man in Yellow, walked
into the woods hand in hand,
lovers grieving their daughter. They buried it under a stone
where no one would find it, taking care of Una's father
once and for all.

Full of anger, Tessa and her lover together concocted a
plan. When the time was right, they would avenge their
daughter's death. Not today, not tomorrow, but one day in
the future they would act when least expected. They would
bring a plague to the town, the town that turned their
backs on their daughter. And if all else fails, he taught her

the command that would call up the fair folk and creatures from the wood as a last resort.

Spirits of the wood
Fair folk hear my plea
I offer you blood of the guilty
Feast, drink and be free

She peeked into baby Una's room to see her sleeping soundly. "Oh my poor sweet darling, I will avenge your mother. I will make them all pay," declared Tessa.

"Even if it's the very last thing I do. Not even death will stop me..."

The Origin of the Three Mothers

I was deeply inspired by Gemma Gary and her book The Black Toad a collection of west country witchcraft based in Cornwall and Devon. There were three main chapters entitled Old Mother Red-Cap, Old Mother Green-Cap, and Old Mother Black-Cap. Each of these chapters broke down the use of practical charms, spells, curatives, and curses. The chapter Old Mother Red-Cap depicted an iconic figure whose gifts were versed in charms and spells. The chapter Old Mother Green-Cap contains plant curatives and magic. The chapter Old Mother Black-Cap taught curses, bindings, and the sinistral arts. No name or specificity was given to these three archetypes, so I set out to give them their own stories and build figures that not only educate in magic but also give these archetypal teachers a voice, a spirit, and an identity. Reference part III of this book to learn the magic of the Three Mothers and know they always come to those who ask for aid.

II. Cunning Rhymes:
Magic in Verse

1. Cunning Oil

A witch seeks to know
We twist and we toil
A witch slips between worlds
With a most cunning oil

This oil this grease
Does slip and slide
From here to the hedge
Anointed to glide

On skin and on tools
Or on candle wax
Spellbound lubrication
For a magical climax

The recipe can vary
From land to land
It all depends
On what's at hand

Let me share with you one most potent
You may make it your own of course
Let it be your most cunning oil
A spirit-laden magical source

At first the most important
A bit of witching herb
Atropa belladonna
Or Datura is superb

Next the spirit of artemisia
A weed to pierce the veil
Gatekeeper of dreams and prophecy
Weaver of your new tale

And now the scarlet force
The crimson sap is best
Crushed Dragons Blood
To fully manifest

And now the ritual ash
From your hearth or altar pyre
To feed the holy grip
And twist your new desire

And at last the starry seeds
Amount be three times three
As one does will it
It so now shall it be

A cup of carrier oil
Over a double boiler it must go
And steep for two to four hours
Extracting steady and slow

If heat be not available
In a jar all items be placed
And store from Moon to Moon
As the spirits extract encased

Then do triple strain
On the evening of the full moon
Your witches oil now ready
The sap of magic's womb

Cunning Oil Creation:

An oil to be used in magical workings to anoint skin,
candles, tools, etc. Created
-One cup base oil
-1 Tbsp Belladonna leaves/berries and/or datura seeds
(depending on access)
-3 Tbsp Mugwort and/or wormwood (depending on
access)
-1 Tbsp Crushed Dragons blood resin
1 Tbsp. Ritual ash
9-star anise

Hot extraction: When the moon is full, double boil for 2-4
hours and triple strain through a cheesecloth to store in a
dark bottle or jar.
Cold extraction: Place all items in a jar and seal tight. Shake
daily and keep at hearth or altar for a full moon cycle.
Then triple strain through cheesecloth to store in a dark
bottle or jar.

On the night of its creation or finalization, at your altar or
workspace, draw a circle with your finger or wand around
it in a dextral/clockwise manner then say aloud:

This oil this grease
Does slip and slide
From here to the hedge
Anointed to glide
From above and below
By the spirits of my land
I consecrate this oil
To be a guiding hand

Tap it 3 times with your wand or finger to finish.

Use this oil in magical workings as an all-purpose witching oil. Use it to conjure magic from the powerful spirits within. Anoint candles, sigils, tools, or even yourself with this oil as a way of laying on a team of magical allies.

Author's note: You'll notice this oil is mentioned in part III, chapter 5. When creating this oil, a clever witch might make two batches, one with Dragons Blood, and one without. Then the oil without the Dragons Blood could be used to fashion the flying ointment described in the aforementioned chapter.

2. An Elixir of Protection

A witch consorts with spirits
We twist magic in either direction
Which is why it's most important
A witch has sufficient protection

Wards up for your home
Your land knows you by name
Items worn that guard you
If a hex towards you takes aim

No witch should be without protection
Not a moment of day or night
Once you've spoken with the spirits
They have you in their sight

Come one and come all
Whether invited it matters not
A witches power is a beacon
To the spirits you have brought

And so protect yourself you must
This can be done in many ways
With amulets or talismans
Or with a truly cunning phrase

This potion, this elixir
Can be used for your protection
So make haste to brew this essence
To add to your collection

In a jar add root of Angelica
Black salt, vervain, and rosemary
One bay leaf and dragons blood resin
Oil of pine and leaves of blackberry

Now the liquid for this potion
Just a splash of full-moon water
Then fill to the top with vodka
This elixir shall not falter

Before closing the lid to soak
Your command it must obey
Into the jar do whisper
The cunning words you must say:

Protective spirits
Defensive elixir
Safeguarded by
This enchanted mixture

Then close the lid tight
Trap your intention within
Then for one full moon cycle
Let the extraction begin

The liquid coaxes out the spirit
Allies that protect you
Shake daily as it steeps
This red apotropaic brew

From full moon to full moon
Let it soak and macerate
Till the day it's time to strain
On its finalizing date

This scarlet potion
In an amber bottle pour
To keep out ne'er-do-wellers
Place a few drops at your door

Anoint a ring or a necklace
With a few drops of this essence
To protect you from ill wishes
Or a dark spirit's presence

A few drops in the hearth
To guard you in a working
Your spell wards now set
No nefarious shades lurking

For all-purpose protection
For you this potion will serve
Create with great care
Yourself you must preserve

Elixir Creation:

-1 tsp Angelica root
-1 tsp rosemary
-1 tsp blackberry leaf
-1 tsp black salt
-1 tsp vervain
-1 bay leaf
-A teaspoon of crushed dragons blood
-3 drops of pine essential oil
-A splash of full-moon water
-Vodka

Place the ingredients into a small jar except for the Pine Essential Oil and fill to the top with the vodka. Before closing, whisper into the jar:

Protective spirits
Defensive elixir
Safeguarded by
This enchanted mixture

Triple strain a full moon cycle later (4 weeks) add the Pine Essential Oil and bottle for future use.

It may be used for personal protection by anointing an item or yourself with this elixir. It may also be used for remote protection by adding a few drops onto a picture of your target and chanting the incantation 9 times. Then burn it for strong swift short-term protection or bury it at the roots of an old oak for more accumulative long-term protection.

A note on substitutions: if all herbs listed are not available, I suggest using at least 3 and or using plants with the virtue of protection local to you. Rubbing alcohol or white vinegar can be substituted for the vodka if needed.

3. Crossroad Nails

I journey to the crossroads
A hammer in my hand
An intersection of ways
A place of liminal land

Be it crossroads of three or four
A post there you will see
And in that post will be nails
Old and rusty will they be

Take your hammer and set them free
Collect them for your tools
Keep them safe and treat with respect
These nails are for no fools

Blessing

Crossroads nails are magic
They carry blessing and bane
Two nails crossed and bound in red
Protects you from the profane

Bury at the corners
Of your land and home
To ward from maleficium
Safety within the gloam

A blessing for a newborn babe
Crossed nails bound in red
Left beneath the cradle
Right below the head

The nail from a crossroads
Driven in the hilt of a stang or wand
Will draw on the liminal power
From the cross-quarter ways and beyond

Place a nail in a pillow of lavender
Vervain and mugwort
Place under your head to banish
All nightmares of all sorts

Place a crossroads nail with calendula,
Star anise, and leaf of strawberry
In a charm bag of scarlet red
To win in court cases do carry

To heal an ill person
A taglocked doll be made
Of water, flour, and salt
And healing herbs to aid

Drive a crossroads nail
Into the ailing body part
Of the taglocked doll
Healing spirits do impart

Bane

A bovine tongue sliced open
And a gossips birthdate and name
Placed inside and sewn up
Will make their words go lame

Take to a crossroads outside of town
Or a tree deep in the woods
And wrathfully nail with all your might
To a post or tree hard and good

Then turn around and walk away
Don't you dare look back
Not a wise word about you
Will your spellbound target crack

Take a potato, an onion, or a bovine heart
Inside place the name and birthdate
Of your greatest mortal enemy
For whom you feel nothing but hate

Sew it shut with red thread
Lock your target deep inside
You may use clothing, hair, or nails
Should your foe kindly provide

Take thirteen crossroads nails
And drive them deep into the heart
With each nail driven in say nothing
Only loathing and malice impart

Then take to an old graveyard
Leave two silver coins at the gates
And bury at the northernmost corner
An early grave for your foe now awaits

So journey to the crossroads
To get nails for blessing or bane
The craft of the wise and cunning
Who call upon the old ones' names

I journey to the crossroads
A hammer in my hand
An intersection of ways
My place of liminal land

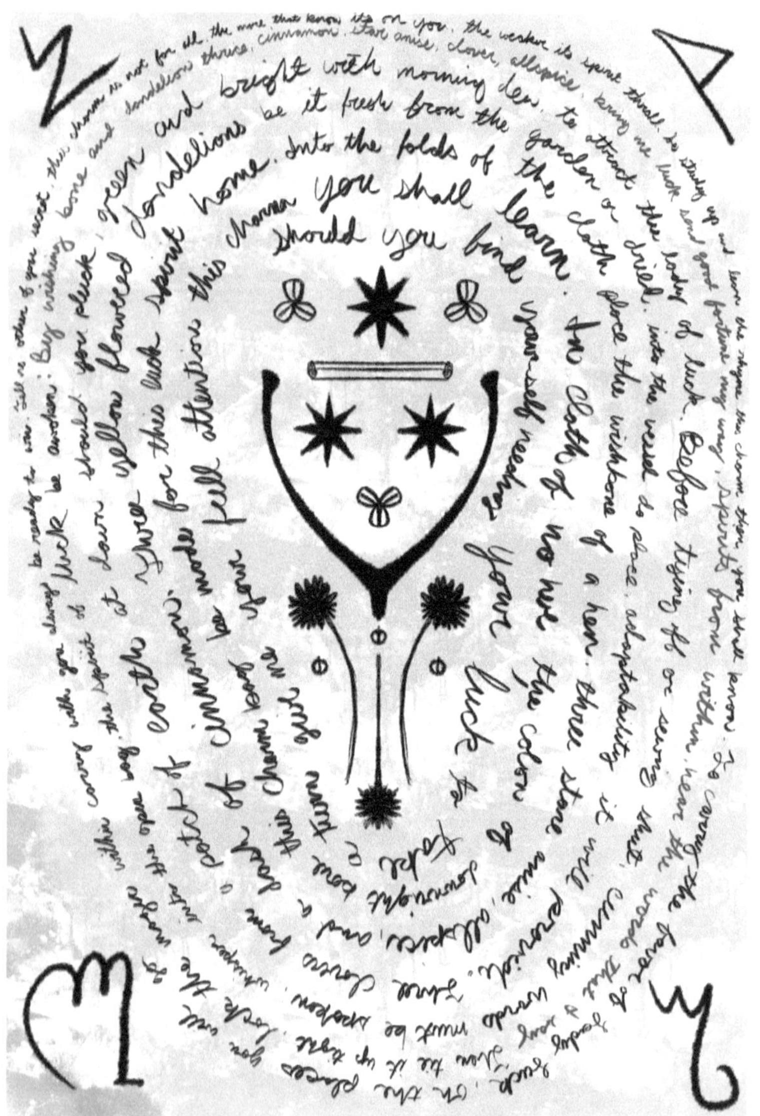

4. A Lucky Charm

Should you find yourself needing
Your luck to take a turn
Give me your full attention
This charm you shall learn

In cloth of no hue
The color of downright bone
This charm bag be made
For this lucky spirit home

Into the folds of the cloth
Place the wishbone of a hen
Three star anise, allspice,
And a dash of cinnamon

Three yellow flowered dandelions
Be it fresh from the garden or dried
Into the vessel do place
Adaptability it will provide

Three clovers from a patch of earth
At dawn should you pluck
Green and bright with morning dew
To attract the lady of luck

Before tying off or sewing shut
Cunning words must be spoken
Whisper into the open bag
The spirit of luck be awoken:

By Wishing bone
And dandelion thrice
Cinnamon, Star Anise,
Clover, Allspice

Bring me luck
Send good fortune my way
Spirits from within
Hear the words that I say

Then tie it up tight
Lock the magic within
Carry with you always
Be ready to win

Tell no other of your secret
This charm is not for all
The more that know it's on you
The weaker its spirit thrall

So study up and learn the rhyme
This charm then you shall know
To carry the favor of Lady Luck
Oh the places you shall go

Charm Instructions:

Items you'll need:
-Charm bag of white
-Chicken wishbone
-3 clovers
-3 dandelion heads
-3 star anise
-Cinnamon
-Allspice

Place all the spell items into the charm bag, whisper into it the charm, and immediately tie up tight. Carry with you.

By Wishing bone
And dandelion thrice
Cinnamon, Star Anise,
Clover, Allspice
Bring me luck
Send good fortune my way
Spirits from within
Hear the words I say

5. Bindweed

Morning glory morning glory
the flower of dewy dawn
Blooming between night and day
A betwixt in-between spirit song

Moonflower Moonflower
Up the trellis vines run
From seed to sky you grow
And bloom at the setting sun

Upon first glance these vines you see
Are beautiful to behold
But then the vines stretch further out
Upon the garden it takes hold

Every other flower, shrub, and bush
Will slowly shrink right back
As the vines quickly take over
And the garden fades to black

Respect these mighty vines
As they reveal their blessing and bane
By bloom and aggressive sprout
They share with you their true name

Bindweeds we are, they sing
We bloom between dark and light
We bring beauty and the spark of spirit
Or a binding chokehold so tight

The flowers can aid your magic
The vines will bind your foe
Listen carefully to this verse
It's important that you know

For candle spells, crush petals
Of morning glory and moonflower
Anoint in oil and roll around
To lend its liminal power

Add to spells or charm bags
For a magical increase
For beauty, love, and success
For harm or for peace

The vines be cut and wound
Around a taglock of your foe
Be it doll with hair and nails
Their name and birthdate you must know

Be it item of clothing or picture,
Signature or handwriting,
As long as it does the job
Of taglock and target uniting

As you wind, sing out this verse
3 times chant as you go
Round around and roundabout
The spell do you sew:

I bind you (name)
I bind you from causing harm
May this weed hold you back
Bound tightly by this charm

Then lock it away somewhere safe
Someplace it won't be found
And your foe shall stay under your spell
As long as they are bound

This spirit of earth so tricky
Morning glory and moonflower
Its name you shan't soon forgot
Bindweed and its mighty power

Glorious Charms and Twisted Bindings

A Glamor Charm Bag

Items needed:
-A pink or purple charm bag
-Morning Glory flowers dried
-3 Datura seeds or Grains of Paradise
-A small young Magnolia pine cone or magnolia flower petals if necessary. If neither of these are available to you, Gardenias or Rose petals could be used.
-A small slip of paper and a pen

On a Friday, write the following words on the paper.

<u>Attractive, Beautiful, Desirable, Vibrant, Confident, Proud, Humble</u>

Feel free to add or subtract traits you feel fit your design. Fold up the paper and place it inside the charm bag along with the other items and say the following charm 7 times into the opening. Close right after the final verse and carry with you to be perceived as beautiful and glamorous.

Fair as Venus
For all to see
A veil of glamour
So shall it be

Ipomoea Breakthrough Evocation

Items needed:
-Dried Morning Glory and/or Moon Flower (Ipomoea)
-Cunning oil or olive oil
-A white chime candle
-A small slip of paper and a pen

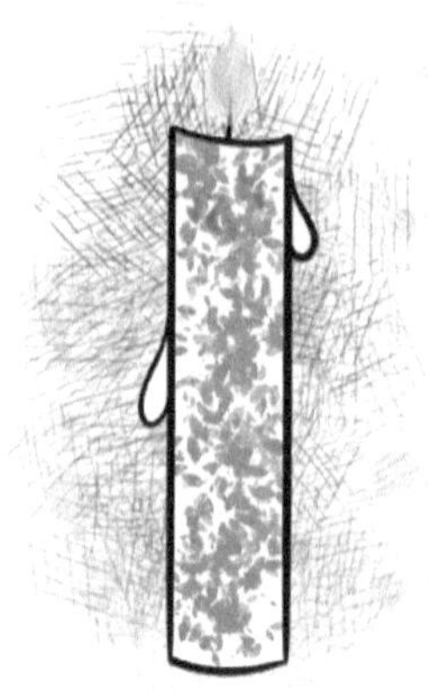

This candle spell will allow you to beseech the spirit of bindweed. Bindweed's ability to creep into spaces and take over give it quite the invasive essence. This determined plant can aid you in breaking through barriers and removing blockages from your path. On the slip of paper, write down the barrier or blockage in your way. Anoint the candle in Cunning oil or olive oil and dress the candle in crushed dried Morning Glory and/or Moon Flowers. Light the candle and say the following chant 100 times or more to create a trancelike state to evoke the spirit of Ipomoea.

Ih Puh Mee Uh

After the final chant, burn the paper in the candle flame and let the candle burn down.

Binding One from Causing Harm

Items needed:
-A fresh-cut vine of Morning Glory or Moon Flower
-A poppet with a taglock of your target inside (hair, nails, signature or handwriting, or a very small personal item). A picture of your target can be used if necessary.

Should you have someone in your life who is causing you strife or harm, bind them by wrapping the fresh-cut vine around the poppet and chanting the charm 13 times.

I bind you (name)
I bind you from causing harm
May this weed hold you back
Bound tightly by this charm

Once done, keep this spelled object in a safe place. To unbind them, cut the vines and douse the poppet or picture in Witches Black Salt and/or Nettles/Rue/Hyssop.

Author's note: If the season or your climate does not allow for Bindweed to thrive, this binding spell can be done with red or black embroidery thread if needed. Just substitute the word "weed" for "thread" to adjust the verbiage.

6. Song of the Cicada

Song of the deafening cicada
Sing to me your southern wiles
Song of the cacophonous cicada
Sing to me of your earthly trials

From the ground do you crawl
From Grubb to winged beast
From larva beneath the darkened earth
To tree tops to make a musical feast

From tree to tree, and Shrub to bush
Winged creature strike your chords
Liminal being of above & below
Sing the aria of the crossroadian Lords

Your fallen comrade here I bury
Amongst the roots of this fine tree
Respectfully cloaked in my desire
Cicada sing out your soul now free

I offer the sap of the maple tree
In a bargain struck here and now
Wings do flicker, rattles sing out
Seeds of this spell do plow

From here to there, and there to yonder
The ballad of the south do they sing
Carry out my will and make it true
My desire now real from song & wing

Southern force, Hear my call
Sing out and loud and clear
Melodic Spirit of my landscape
Cast out my desire. Bring it here!

A Petition to the Cicada

Should you find a deceased cicada carcass, save it for this spell. Write your reasonable desire on paper and wrap it around the cicada's body. Burry it in the roots of an old tall tree where other cicadas dwell. Pour over maple syrup as an offering to the cicadas of your landscape and speak the full cunning rhyme. As the cicadas croak for their lost sibling, they will take your offering and sing out. As the song travels, it will set in motion the reality of your desire.

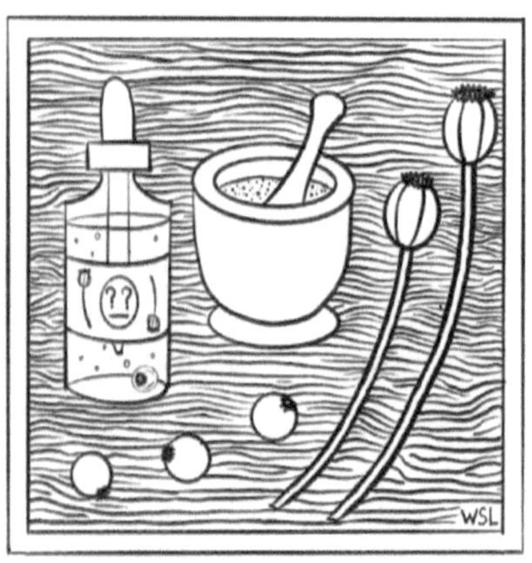

7. Befuddled

The cunning are clever
The cunning know what we should
We know when our foes
Are too smart for their own good

We know the art of the land and sea
We know the art of potion making
By book, by spirit, by seed and berry
Our targets wisdom is for the taking

Add three blueberries into a jar
Dark amber glass is best to use
History teaches they were to be cast
At the door of those you wished to confuse

Then seeds of the poppy
Only just a teaspoon
These little black allies
For the mind spell doom

Then some black witches salt
Made of ritual ash from your altar
Grind together with salt of the sea
And this elixir shall not falter

Then add a splash of dark moon water
That once sat out under the black sky
A starscape of darkness no moon be seen
From dusk till dawn, water so light shy

Then fill with spirits. Vodka works well
Into the jar's dark amber glass
Then seal shut and shake daily
Till four to six weeks has past

Then strain into a glass dropper bottle
But before closing there's one thing more
Speak the cunning words below
This spoken charm do implore:

Berry befuddle
Bewildering seed
Salt noir
Confused indeed

Then close up tight and keep it safe
Label well to not misuse
This elixir is not for petty wiles
Do not overreach and abuse

To confuse and befuddle your foe
There are several ways this can be done
Add a few drops to food or beverage
Or remotely this spell can be spun

A few drops on a personal item
Hair, nails, clothes, or a picture,
You could even use their handwriting
To anoint with this baneful mixture

Just say the cunning words above
Whisper ever so slyly the chant
As you add the drops of the elixir
Confusion you will implant

This spell will last for a single day
Use against the unfair and unjust
Twenty-Four hours of this befuddling elixir
So use wisely as you feel you must

The Elixir and Spell:

In a small jar add:
-3 macerated Blueberries
-1Tsp. Poppyseeds
-1Tsp, Black witches salt
-Fill with vodka & a splash
of Dark moon water

Strain 4-6 weeks later into a dark
glass dropper bottle. Before closing,
whisper into the bottle this chant
and shut tight:

Berry befuddle
Bewildering seed
Salt noir
Confused indeed

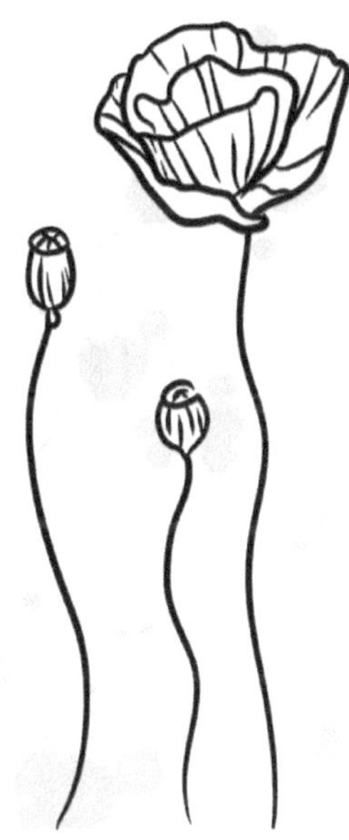

Whenever using for a spell to cause confusion and
befuddlement, recite the charm as you sprinkle a few drops
at the doorway of your target or on a taglock of them (hair,
clothing, picture, name paper) do not put in someone's
food or drink without consent. That would be positively
wicked.

8. Climatic Sigil

Sigils are a magical glyph
Created with your intent
A statement broken down
Till a symbol does present

The letters may be used
Any which way you prefer
You may remove vowels and doubles
However they may occur

You may use the statement alone
To draw what it does inspire
The spirit of your statement
A symbol of your desire

There are many ways to use this glyph
It can be buried or it can burn
It can be carried or used in spells
The art of the sigil you now learn

But there is one method
And it's most taboo
This method does require
Your most personal brew

Your sigil be drawn
On paper with care
Then arouse yourself
If you do so dare

With a partner or more
May this working be done
Or all on your own
One touch and it's begun

Work yourself up
A sweat should you break
With stimulation and fervor
Sex magic you make

Faster and faster
Great tension do build
The eruption to come
Desire soon fulfilled

Once you reach release
All attention as you quake
Directed at your sigil
As you cum it does awake

With eyes on the tiny symbol
Till the last spasm of pleasure
This energy transference
A massive trove of treasure

And finally to finish
Just one thing more to know
The fluid you excrete
On the sigil it must go

What you do with it after
Is totally up to you
Let it dry on your altar
Or up your chimney flue

In your book of spells
It may also go
A place to record the outcome
Jotted just below

Just don't go and destroy it
Oh no, not just yet
Give it time to work for you
Wait and don't you fret

Though if you find the results
Not quite up to your desire
If it goes awry or wonky
Circumstances aren't most dire

Just soak in sea salt and water
Till the sigil does dissolve
With hyssop, rue, and nettle
The spell on its own will devolve

The sigil of the unspoken
Now written here to see
The magic of the orgasm
By the cunning used wisely

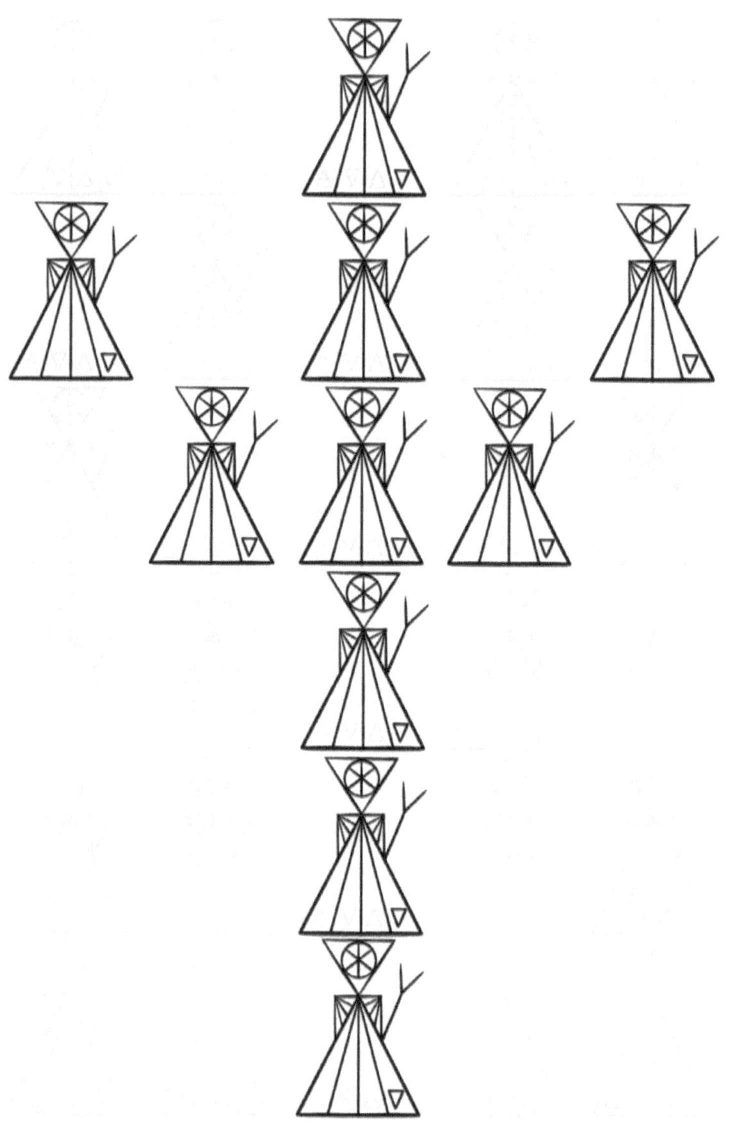

9. Petition to the Oak

On a scroll of paper
you must write
Your desire
rolled up tight

Bound and tied
thrice by thread
Color of crimson
Life's blood red

One end of this thread
Three holly berries be
Gathered from thy land
At sunrise picked by thee

On the other end
Do snake bones be
By chain of spine
Serpent vertebrae three

One thing more
And all is done
Venture out
At set of sun

Bury the scroll
At twilight hour
In oaken roots
The tree of power

Offer up hair
Or blood or seed
A part of you
the Oak does need

Upon sunrise
The spell be done
The tree's magic
Has now begun

10. The Gift of the Paper Doll

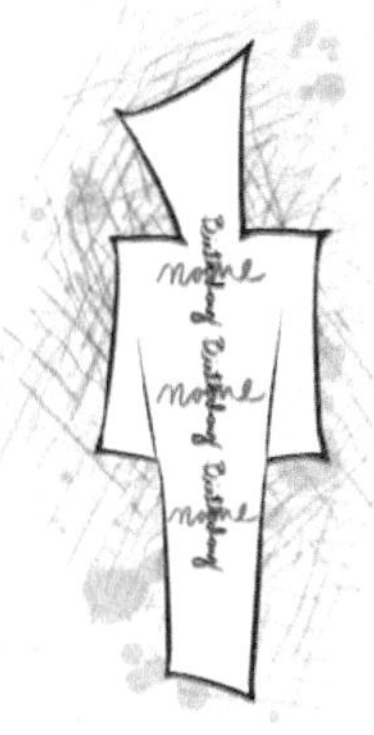

Name and birth written
On a Doll made of paper
In a cross three times
Going down the center

Say the words
To twist and bind
And take control
Of fate's design

My paper doll
Now christened be
Target be bound
To my will of thee

To bind one who's crossed you
Doll of paper be rolled
Bound in red thread
While this chant
be doled

Thread be wrapped
Scarlet to bind
Harm me you may not
My words you shall mind

To bind one who's crossed you
Doll of paper be rolled
Bound in red thread
While this chant be doled

Thread be wrapped
Scarlet to bind
Harm me you may not
My words you shall mind

This sigil be drawn
If health be stricken
on the body part
With the affliction

This sigil be drawn
On the dominant hand
To attract money
Upon thy command

If love be desired
On the heart you must write
The sigil of love
To attract your mates sight

To silence a tongue
speaking words so malicious
Sew their lips shut
To block their ill wishes

The Rite

Within a drawn circle
And angles of three
Lay down the poppet
And grasp reality

Over the doll
A candle do place
Light a flame
And chant at pace

Spirits of old
Aid me this hour
Sigil spirit forces
Lend me your power
Bound paper doll
In image of thee
My will be done
So shall it be

13 times round
Or till flame be done
The more times spoken
The more power spun

Upon the conclusion
Keep the doll hidden
From those who would recoil
At the art of the forbidden

Now one more lesson
For circumstances most dire
This doll's to be burned
At your altar pyre

To bring someone bad tidings
Mark their eyes crossed
They be pricked with a thorn
And burnt till flame lost

As the fire consumes
This now cursed doll
Chant backwards their name
Envisioning their fall

The craft of the doll
You now do know
The gift of the poppet
To you now bestowed

Authors note: These sigils were created by me of my own method. Should you feel your symbols or style of sigil-making is better for you, feel free to substitute and expand on this versatile spell. It is designed in a way to simplify and streamline a poppet spell using a paper doll. Once the doll is bound to your target by name and birthdate it is christened and the sigil drawn on it carries the desire within. The rite listed above allows for a single ritual that can activate all of the given sigils. Place the doll in the center of a circle and triangle as drawn above, place the candle over the doll and light it. Chant the incantation 13 times or more should it suit your practice.

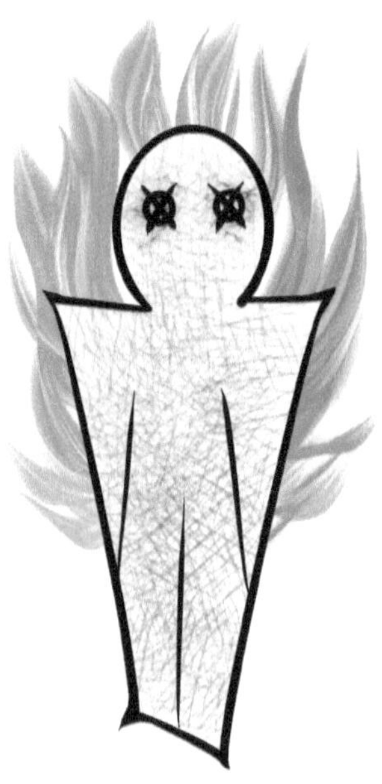

11. The Wrathful River Spirits

A young man went down to the river
The cooling water he sought.
One black eye, a broken rib,
Hold his tears back, he could not

The look on his father's face
The hatred in his eyes
As he beat his son for catching him
Between the Stablehand's thighs

On his bruises he pressed cool water
From the rapid flowing river
He breathed a sigh from deep within
Relief the water delivered

Anger seethed within him
The pain becoming unbearable
His gut ached and turned
From his father's words so terrible

"You're not my son, you queer.
Be gone and never return!
You're dead to me & your mother too,
Her ashes are turning in her urn!"

How could he be so heartless
To his one and only son
How could he take back his love
His whole world had come undone

Child of liminal nature,
we hear your cries of pain
We spirits of the river
For here is where we reign

The young man stood back from the water
as the river spirits' words flowed out
"How can you help?" He asked
"What can I do?" Did he shout

Give us your assailant's name and birthdate
In a poppet to empower
Made of earth and wood
At the twilight sunset hour

Into the mud, mix as follows:
Nettles, black salt, and nightshade
An item from your target
Some twigs and it is made

Toss the likeness into our embrace
And we'll take him into the deep
Now wipe your tears, son of Aradia
From this day no more shall you weep

Under moonlight he made his way
to the cottage of the Stablehand
And that night they worked together
They plotted and they planned

They made a doll as instructed
With a scrap of his father's necktie
And at dusk to the river they went
The poppet cloaked from curious eyes

At the rocky river's edge
The rapids raged cold and wet
They held hands as they tossed the doll
Into the angry river's depths

The horizon flashed as the sun set
And the poppet sank below
A roar came crashing up
The wild river spirits in tow

Upon the surface of the water
An image spiraled about
And they saw his father's face
The light in his eyes going out

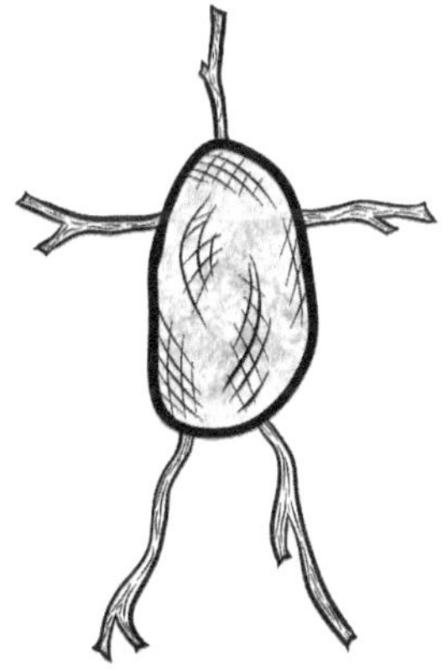

They braved the journey home
To his father's manor did they go
Upon arrival they saw the gift
The river spirits did bestow

"Drowned in the bathtub," they said
In only three feet of water
Drunk on wine, he slipped and hit his head
His own self did he slaughter

The son once turned out and broken
Now the master of his fate
He finally had all he ever wanted
His health, a safe home, and his mate

. . .

All hail the river spirits
Mighty, powerful, and cruel
This song I sing to conjure them
This chant be your blessed tool

Sing the rhyme and verse
As you cast out your taglocked doll
Then turn around and don't look back
And await your enemy's fall

12. Invoking the Witch's Devil and Witch Queen

Write your reasonable desire on a small slip of paper and follow the invocation.

I call upon the Horned One
The Great initiator
Hail the Man in Black
Witch King and Gatekeeper

Spirit of the physical realm
Serpent of my land
Granter of knowledge, Genius Loci
Meet me where I stand

Mark this place a crossroads
Between all time and space
Cross-quarter ways be open
The other world I embrace

The Horned One be one with me
Witch Father take my hand
I invoke the Man in Black
The Devil of my land

Lady of Other
Between time and space
Above and below
A liminal place

Mother of heaven
Queen of hell
Betwixt and between
Where magic does dwell

She who holds the threads
The weaver of all fate
She who sees all ways
Who creates and can unmake

Goddess of the moon and stars
And void of the unseen
Across the hedge sits the throne
Of this our Witch Queen

One with my body
One with my mind
Feel what I feel
Our desired entwined

I send up this task
Bind it to your will
Witch King and Witch Queen
My petition fulfill

*Add a fingerprint to the petition stamped in a drop of your blood,
and say:*

Anointed with blood
My payment to thee
Offered up by fire
My desire to be

*Burn the petition till it is ash and give the spirits license to depart
with the following words*

.

From my body now depart
Released from my mind
By the light between the horns
This spell do now bind

And clap loudly to end

Author's note: In some forms of traditional witchcraft, there is a system of archetypal spirits represented by a Witch King and Witch Queen. These energies have been called many names: Witch Father, Horned One, Man in Black, Witch's Devil, the Witch Mother, the Goddess, and my personal favorite Lady of Other. I think it's really important to break down a few misconceptions about this perceived dichotomy. These are not the traditional Lord and Lady from Wicca. These are not representative of the Divine Masculine or Divine Feminine in a gender-oriented way. In my practice, these are two sides of a whole and everything in between. They represent ideas and archetypes that have always existed long before humankind. I'm not talking about a documented pantheon or the debunked Witch Cult of Western Europe theory. I'm talking about the makeup of our reality. The Witch King represents the physical and Witch Queen represents the nonphysical. I equate them to Physicality and Desire from the Preface of this book as primordial forces. I very much see the Man in Black, the Witch's Devil, the Witch Father, the Horned One as the Physical gatekeeper to the nonphysical, and the Witch Queen to the spark of Desire. They are not just binary beings as they exist separately but also together, like the body and the soul, the earth and the gravity that pulls it, the tangible and intangible. So please do not reduce these enigmatic figures to representations of gender or cycles of fertility. They represent the queerness of liminality and so much more.

13. The Red Meal

On the day of the thirty-first
On October's final night
A special feast is made
A witches' offering rite

At a place of sacred space
A glass of wine blood red
Given to the spirits
And a loaf of fresh dark bread

Call in the Crossroadian Lords
The spirits of your court
Those who have come and gone
And their land and sky cohorts

The Red Meal is a thanks
And communion with in between
A Housle Cochrane coined
For those who go unseen

Speak the cunning words
And let them know of your boon
The following prayer send out
And with the spirits commune:

Happy Halloween!
Happy Samhain!
Happy All Hallows' Eve!
The dead are alive
The veil is thin
We don masks to deceive

A liminal time
The witches' new year
High magic do we weave
The devil dances
The Witch mother does sing
All one must do is believe

We break the bread
We sip the wine
Hollowed blessings we receive
And for the spirits
Of above and below
An offering we leave

A bite of bread, a sip of wine
Into your soul do take
And leave the rest for ones of old
And dead to partake

No more shall it remain there
Longer than a day times three
Then give it back to the land
At a crossroads or where dead be

And remember this yearly rite
Remember those who came before
Remember those we loved and lost
And honor the spirits once more.

III. Cunning Compendium:
a Codex of Grimoires, Rites, and Extrapolated Charms, Spells, and Curses

Preface:
The Magic Square of the Old Ones

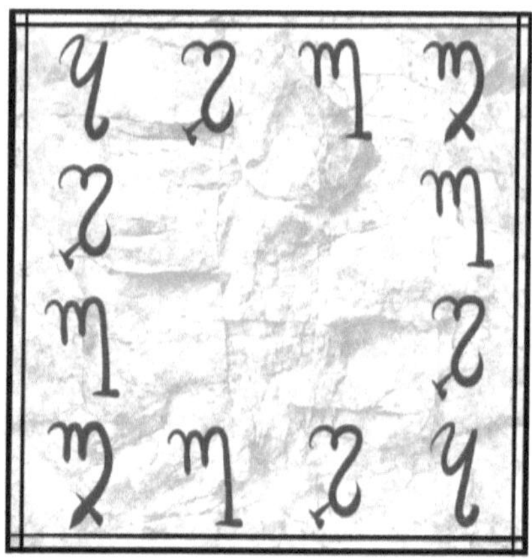

This square is a type of palindrome that conjures the Old Ones as seen in the Preface: Absence, Existence, Desire, and Physicality. They represent the archetypal spirits that make up the material of this universe. Absence is the void of nothingness. Existence is the first spark of time and space. Desire is the want, the need for more. And Physicality is that desire made real. The first letters of each Old One line up backward and forwards in Theban to create a perfect square. Carry this square with you as a talisman of magic, add it to charm bags, or write your petitions in the center to evoke the energies of the Old Ones.

Of Water, Salt, and Dirt

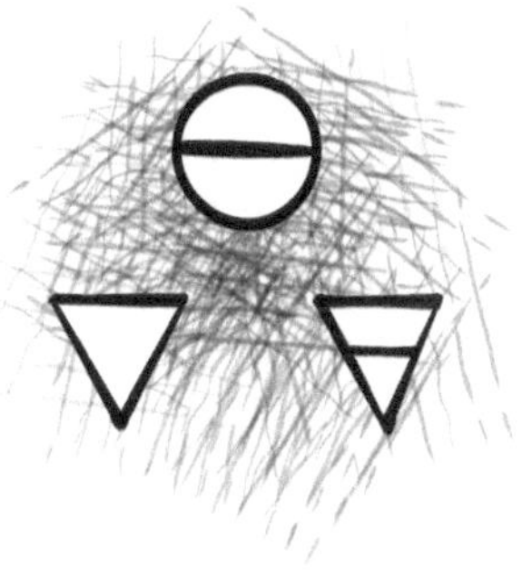

Full Moon Water
Items needed:
-Fresh clean water
-A resealable glass jar or bottle

On the night of the full moon, fill the jar or bottle with water and go outside or to a window. Hold out the vessel towards the sky. If you can view the moon through the water, this is an added advantage. Say the incantation and leave the vessel out overnight. Be sure to take it in before the sun rises and light touches it.

Full moon high above
Brightening the sky
Charge this water here
Make the magic mine
Bless this with your power
Imbued by your decree
Tide maker and tide breaker
Sealed waters of destiny
So shall it be

Full moon water is a multifaceted tool for witches and because of its simplicity, it is often scoffed at. Make no mistake, this is a simple, accessible spirit ally. It can be used in water magic, offerings, teas, potions, and elixirs to add the potency of the moon at its peak. It can be used to water magical plants or sprinkled to bless a home or space. You'll find several workings include Full Moon Water within this book.

Dark Moon Water

Items needed:
-Fresh clean water
-A resealable glass jar or bottle

While Full Moon Water captures the potency of the full moon, Dark Moon water bottles its absence. Carry out the same procedure as before but this time hold your vessel up towards the dark sky to show only blackness through the glass and say the following incantation. Leave the vessel out overnight and bring it indoors before sunrise.

This particular charged water can be used for more sinistral activities. It can be used in potions, teas, tonics, and items consumed meant to carry baneful intentions. It can also be used as an offering in necromancy or to chthonic deities. Be sure to keep this water covered and in the dark. It shall see no more than candlelight otherwise risks losing its potency.

Witch's Black Salt

Items Needed:
-1 part sea salt
-1 part ritual/hearth ash
(Ash built up from previous ritual incense,
burnt offerings, or cooled coal from a ritual fire)
-Mortar and pestle

This is a multifaceted tool for witches. It carries with it the virtues of protection, warding, and hex-making and breaking. Salt represents sacredness and purity, a crystalline structure that can cleanse and consecrate. The ash comes from burnt offerings and incinerated intentions in the form of grey and black soot. Embers that once offered light and heat, now a ghost of their former flame. The mixing of these two spirits births the Witch's Black Salt, a cunning and twisted child of light and dark, defense and offense, creating an armor of ashen scars. Black Salt carries with it the time, the energy, and the magic created within the ash. It evokes the virtues of Fire and Air while the salt evokes the virtues of Earth and Water. To create, grind together alternating clockwise and counterclockwise while chanting the cunning words:

Black salt of ash
Black salt of earth
Come together
For this magical birth
Malice, protection,
Banishments, and wards
Witches Black Salt
Be my crossed swords

This is a common spirit ally you can use in multiple ways. Sprinkle it across your doorstep to keep out ill wishes, malefic energies, or undesired spirits. Add it to charms for protection or mix with water to paint sigils on talismans or your home. Use in baneful work or defense magic. In a cauldron, mix in water to affect a target mentally, with dirt from a crossroads to affect them physically, or fire to affect them energetically. You'll find several workings within this very book that require Black Salt.

Author's note: Salt when put into the soil will kill most living organisms leaving the ground barren, so it is suggested never to discard this or any other spell ingredients that include salt in the earth. Instead, respectfully throw it away into the garbage. Should you feel that the earth is where you prefer to discard your spell remains, I suggest switching out salt to ground eggshells. In this case, it would be instead called **Black Ova** (ova means eggs in Latin). Simply adjust the spell incantation from the words *Black Salt* for *Black Ova* to adjust the verbiage.

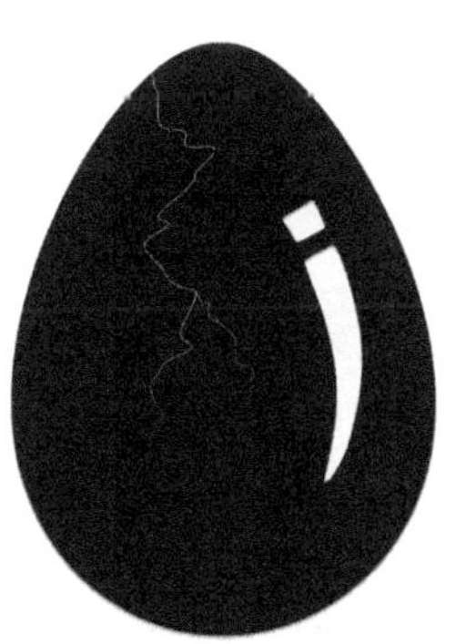

Dirt

The dirt, soil, sand, minerals, mycelium, and very earth beneath our feet is magic. It carries with it virtues, impressions, and energy from what dwells there. Homes, lands, and people are spiritually affected by their experiences. Dirt is no different and it can pick up impressions of the world above. Use the dirt from archetypal places of significance, authority, or power in magic as follows.

Power and Potency: Dirt from a crossroads

Protection: Dirt found at a barrier gate bordering a home or dwelling.

Health: Dirt from a hospital

Financial Gain: Dirt from a bank

Love: Dirt gathered from an outdoor wedding

Education: Dirt from a school

Hearth and Home: Dirt from the land you reside on and ash from your hearth or past ritual incense.

Motivation: Dirt from a gym or activity center

Art: Dirt from a museum

Legal Matters: Dirt from a Courthouse

Pets: Dirt from a veterinary clinic

Necromancy: Dirt from a cemetery (always pay for this by asking and leaving an offering. I suggest two 25-cent coins)

Hexing and Cursing: Dirt from the roots of a poisonous plant or also from a crossroads.

This earth can be carried in charm bags, used in magical powders, or workings of your creation. Get your hands dirty.

These three simple tools are readily available spirit allies. Do not underestimate water, salt, and dirt. For many folk practitioners, that's all they need.

Author's note: The section on dirt is dedicated to Olivia Graves. After several years of friendship, she has become a confidant, a mentor, a shoulder to lean on, and most wonderfully, a fellow witch that I can share my practice with. We both took a class that birthed a love of dirt in magic and it spawned countless conversations that at some point included this very topic. If there's one thing she taught me, it's to get dirty in your craft.

Contracting with an Herbal Familiar

Under the full moon, pick the mature root of a witching herb you have found or nurtured. I suggest a Mandrake, Datura, or Pokeweed root depending on what you have access to. Uproot it at sunset, clean it, and you may even carve a small face if desired. Dry it out in the oven at the lowest setting with the oven door left cracked open for around 2-3 hours or dry naturally in a cool dry place till the following full moon and continue. Then at midnight, give it a drop of your blood from your left pointer finger at its center, a bit of your hair (body hair is acceptable), and then bind it in red embroidery thread. Once wrapped to keep the hair and root system together, tie 13 knots of the same thread around the bound root. With each knot say the following words.

After the final knot, the working is done. Let it rest at your altar, hearth, or workspace overnight. Over the next few days, make it a nice home, maybe in a cared-for box or glass vessel. Get to know your familiar as it's part of your spiritual family now. Does it tell you things it likes? Tell it things about you. Your familiar is your friend and spirit ally. Tell it your desires and send its specter to do your bidding. Maintain a regular feeding schedule of a drop of blood from the left pointer finger once a month on the night of the full moon. Should you stop feeding your familiar, it will stop helping you and the contract will be broken.

Authors note: If you happen to dig up your root to find a cluster of two or three intertwined, keep them together for the spell. They grew together in the earth. Let them work in unison as your familiar. I, myself, used a datura root that had twisted together with its neighbor and grown into a shape that left each root hugging the other with its extended roots. The night I made this contract, I had strange dreams of laying in bed with someone else. We were cuddling face to face, legs and arms wrapped around one another. The feeling wasn't sexual, but comforting, as if I was aligning with the very familiar I had made a convenient with. Pay attention to your dreams once this bargain is struck. Your new familiar might just have something to show you. On the occasion that no roots are available to you, a liminal stone found between land and water may be used. River quartz is best. Just substitute the words "Twisted root" with "Liminal stone."

The Fashioning of Charm Bags and Sachets

There are multiple spells in this book that call for charm bags and there are several ways these can be made. Here are a few examples along with the benefits of each.

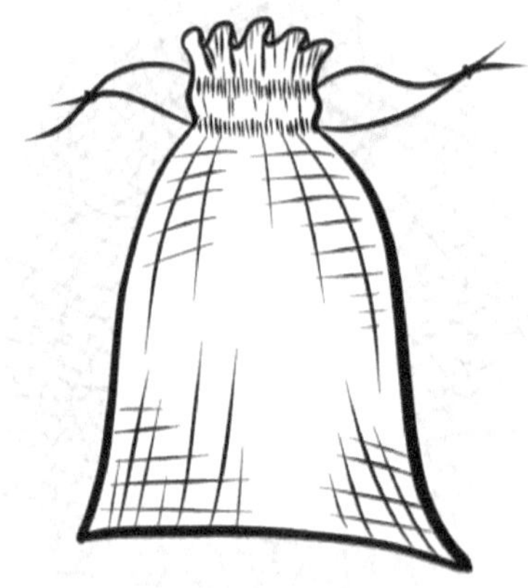

Premade charm bags of different fabrics and colors can be purchased or made by hand with drawstrings at the top to tighten. These are usually accessible and the premade option is the most simple and easy to work with.

A square of fabric can be laid out and all items intended to go inside can be placed in the center. Gather the edges into a bundle and tie off the opening with string to create a sack below. This method is the most accessible but requires slightly more attention to creation.

Fold a rectangle of fabric in half to create a square, and sew up two of the sides leaving a final side open. Fill the opening with the items intended to go within and sew the top edge closed. Sewing takes on an added bit of magic as it allows the

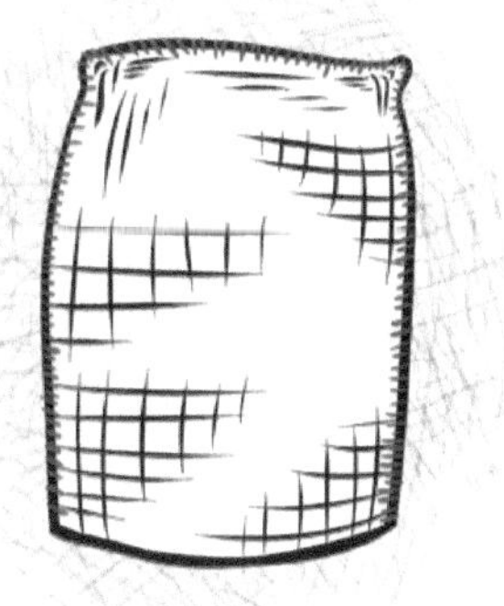

witch to build up energy for the charm. Chanting while sewing builds power. Apply this technique to spells that use charm bags for what I believe adds an energetic increase. This method is accessible but requires the most attention to detail.

A Doll of Dough:
Poppets and Sympathetic Rites

Poppets have been used in sympathetic magic within different cultures around the world. Sympathetic magic is the act of working a spell with items on a smaller scale to imitate the effect you'd like it to have in the world around you. The microcosm affects the macrocosm. Like corresponds with like. So with a doll made in someone's likeness, a witch could work magic on it, and it would sympathetically affect the person it represents.

While the doll itself doesn't have to look like its intended target, it will need to be connected to its real-life counterpart in some way. With poppets, personal items from your target are put inside the doll like hair, nail clippings, handwriting, their signature, a picture, or scroll of paper with their name and birthdate written 3-9 times.

Another aspect of sympathetic magic is the rule of correspondence. This is where certain herbs, stones, and items carry virtues that can be used to specify your intent in spellcraft. A red rose corresponding with romance could be used in love magic. Bay leaves or onion skin in your billfold might correspond with cash to attract money your way. Foxglove corresponds with magic for heart health because the plant is used as a heart medicine called digitalis. Honey corresponds with sweetness so it could be used in charms to make someone or a situation more amiable. Aluminum corresponds with Mercury because it's so malleable. It could be worked with in a charm for open communication, travel, or commerce. This is also why many plants used in baneful magic are highly toxic and poisonous. It's important to understand, this can change from culture to culture. So not all practices will use the same correspondence.

When making a poppet, a witch might put healing herbs inside to work healing magic on their target. They might put coins or herbs that correspond to money to attract prosperity. They might put in flowers or spices that correspond to romance for love magic.

Forming a Poppet of Salt Dough

A very easy way of creating a poppet is with salt dough. The following simple recipe may be used.

-2 parts plain/all-purpose flour
-1 part table salt
-1 part water (full moon or dark moon water could be used here in matters of dextral or sinistral magic)

Mix the flour and salt in a large bowl, followed by the taglock of your target, and any herbs, minerals, metals, or other spirit allies. You can choose to air dry it for several days to firm up, or you can dry it in the oven at its lowest temperature with the oven door left cracked open for 30 minutes to several hours. Dry it to the stiffness of your desire.

Some like to include a ritual to christen the poppet to name and connect it to their target. I feel that simply consecrating a taglocked doll in frankincense or dragon's blood incense smoke while saying the following aloud does well.

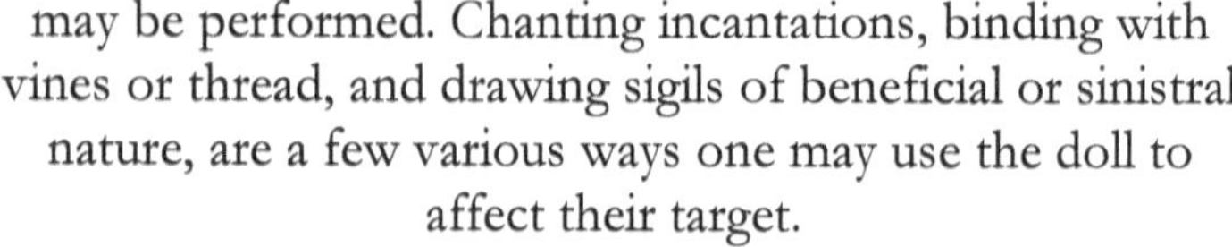

I christen thee (targets name)
I christen thee (targets name)
I christen thee (targets name)

Once your poppet is created and christened, you're desired magic may be performed. Chanting incantations, binding with vines or thread, and drawing sigils of beneficial or sinistral nature, are a few various ways one may use the doll to affect their target.

Pins have long been used in poppet work to heal or harm. Pins placed in the area of the body afflicted with illness while chanting healing charms over it will direct your magic to the problem area. Likewise, pins can be used to harm by chanting curses of bane and pinning specific areas or all over the doll.

To break a spell cast on your poppet, give it a bath of hot water, Nettles, and Witches Black Salt. Hyssop and Rue are also wonderful at breaking spells and hexes. Do not drown the doll but bathe it. An act of easing away the poppet's connection to its real-life counterpart. A statement or chant might be made 13 times while doing this such as:

The doll of dough will become slippery or start to come apart; that's ok. It's desired. Once done, respectfully discard it in the garbage. It's not advised to leave in nature because of the salt and processed flour content.

Flying Ointment

In Part I, chapter 3, the story First Flight tells the tale of spirit flight and an initiation of sorts. The grease the two characters anointed their body with is the infamous flying ointment. It was believed that in ancient times, witches would use a salve to coat their bodies and give them the ability to fly. At one point, there was great discourse during medieval witch trials about whether witches physically flew or their spirits left their bodies to fly in the form of their specters. This is one of the ideas that led to spectral evidence being permitted at witch trials.

Historical records show multiple accounts of flying ointments being created with a manner of poisons and unsavory items like the fat of an unbaptized baby, deadly nightshade, and other toxic plants like mandrake, henbane, datura, and other witching herbs. It was even suggested in *Hallucinogens and Shamanism by Michael J Harner* that the idea of witches flying on brooms came from applying these highly hallucinogenic ointments to broom handles and inserting them into a bodily orifice. He states this would have caused them to have visions of flying. Unfortunately, as exciting as this idea is, there is not sufficient evidence to prove such a claim.

Spirit flight does exist though and has in many forms around the world. In modernity, it's synonymous with astral projection which anyone can do but requires regular practice and skill to achieve. This doesn't look exactly like one might think. It's a very meditative exercise that involves going inward to go outward. The below recipe uses nontoxic herbal allies. For more information about creating or procuring an ointment made with plants from the poison path, see the author's note at the end of this chapter.

Artemisia Flying Ointment Recipe

Items needed:
-1/2 cup of Mugwort and/or Wormwood
-1 cup carrier oil (jojoba, grape seed, or olive oil)

Cold Extraction
Place the herbs and carrier oil in a small jar and seal tightly with as little air as possible. Let a full moon cycle pass (about 4 weeks) to slowly extract the spirit of the plant material and triple strain with a cheesecloth or sieve.

Hot Extraction
Place the herbs and carrier oil in a double boiler and heat for 2-4 hours to extract the spirit of the plant material. Once done, triple strain with a cheesecloth or sieve.

This is a simple nontoxic oil of Artemisia (the species of Mugwort and Wormwood). You may also use the Cunning Oil from Part II, chapter 1, but that might leave a slight reddish stain on the skin and does include a toxic substance. A clever witch might consider that very recipe without the dragon's blood as another option to be made into this ointment. Once the oil base has been created, you may move forward with your ointment. The following ratios are best.

-1 cup of the created oil
-1/4 cup of beeswax

Warm the oil and the wax in a double boiler and pour when hot into a salve tin or small jar and let cool. Always test a small patch of skin to be sure you will not have any allergy or reaction, use sparingly, and do not use if you are pregnant and/or trying to conceive.

Practical Uses

There are several ways a practitioner could be aided with this witches' grease. When holding rituals, casting spells, or preparing for dream work, one might anoint their temples, neck, and/or body to open the self up to the liminal spirits lubricating their magic or communication to the otherworld.

It's also used in traditional spirit flight which is a more involved ritual. Anoint the body at the temples, neck, armpits, groin, and feet about 30 minutes before flight to absorb the ointment through the skin. Then sit comfortably or lay down (but try not to fall asleep) and begin regulating your breath. Four seconds in, four seconds out. Five seconds in, five seconds out. Six seconds in, and six seconds out. Relax the body and notice your heart slowing to relax. Begin chanting if you find it aids you in slipping into a trance. I might suggest the simple words spoken in First Flight.

Allow the words to run together as you chant. Let them become meaningless. In your very relaxed state, envision and feel yourself slipping out of your body. What you do next is not for me to instruct, but for you to experience. You may reach out to spirits, or fly off to the witches' sabbath. You may use this liminal space to contact familiars, the dead, or the divine.

A personal vision that has come to me with the aid of flying ointment: I'm lifted off the ground and sore high into the sky. I find myself landing in a dark wooded area and the trees shroud me creating a private sacred space. Four familiar spirits of the cross-quarter ways come from each direction, the snake of the east, the hare of the south, the toad of the west, and the crow of the north (as written about by Gemma Gary in Traditional Witchcraft). We gather around the center where a natural makeshift altar exists. Here I commune with the spirits, expand upon my gnosis, and work feats of magic.

Author's note: Do not use if you are pregnant or trying to conceive. For more information on working with poisonous plants and flying ointment, I recommend The Poison Path by Coby Michael. Coby writes detailed instructions on creating flying ointment with toxic plants and has an online shop of oils, elixirs, ointments, and more all created from poisonous plants and witching herbs. I'd suggest The Witches Sabbath by Kelden for further research on the sabbath, its origin, history, and a very thorough education on spirit flight with practical exercises.

Chanting the Beads

Beads are a wonderful tool for a witch to use in spell craft because they create a straightforward way to speak your intentions aloud in repetition or evoking spirit aid while keeping track of how many times you've spoken the specific chant. It builds up power, energy, and momentum.

You can purchase a string of simple beads or craft your own. The number of beads is your choice as your craft is based on your education and personal gnosis. Some practitioners work with beads created to only work with specific deities or spirits, and some have a singular set for all-purpose spell craft. Many of the rites in this very book instruct several times a chant should be repeated based on planetary or magical numbers. Below you will find an example structure for all-purpose witch's chanting beads.

Creating the Beads

Items needed:
-57 medium-sized beads (of your color choice)
-62 smaller spacer beads (of your color choice)
-4 large spacer beads
-Nylon beading string or jewelry wire
-A single talisman/pendant of your choice

The setup is similar to a rosary but the number of beads differs. The main necklace consists of 4 sets of 13 medium beads with 4 large beads separating the 4 sections. The pendant hangs on a single strand with 5 medium beads.

Use the spacer beads as desired to separate the medium and larger ones.

The 4 sets of 13 beads represent the 4 cross-quarter ways north, east, south, and west as well as the four corresponding elements air, fire, earth, and water. The number 13 has a long history in superstition and folklore, but in this setting, it represents the 13th hour, the time out of time. It creates a purposeful liminality that defies our 12-hour interpretation and conception of the clock. The 5 beads that lead to the pendant also represent the four elements plus the fifth, Spirit.

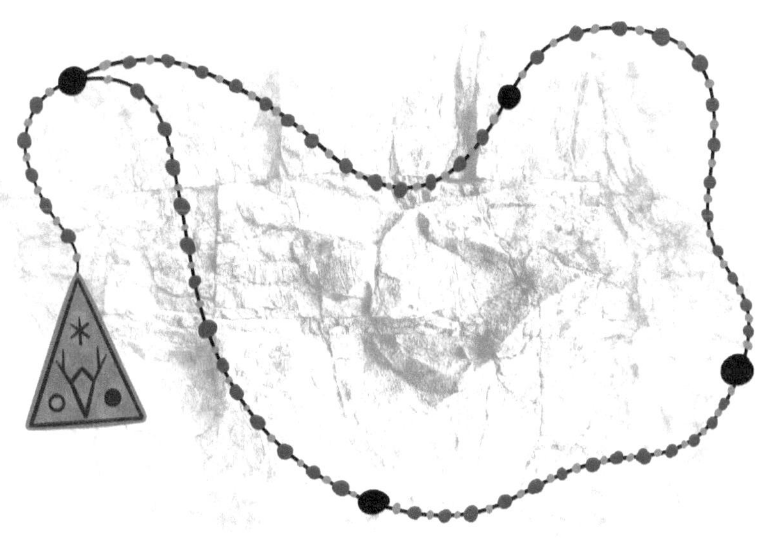

Chanting

To chant the beads, one might create straightforward clear statements to chant over a poppet or candle spell as simple as *I attract prosperity, Heal (full name) of all illness, "I draw forth a lover, Protect (name) from (the dangerous situation at hand).* Start at the pendant and work your way up and around the beads chanting the statement repeatedly till the words run together and your mind slips into a waking trance. This state of mind is still aware but in a more relaxed and in-between space. You may feel that chanting the whole set of beads is best to build the energies required or only a certain number based on astrological or magical correspondences such as planetary numbers as seen in Part III, chapter 13.

Another option is to have a set of chants to use for specific desires. These can be in line with the elements, the planets, or a set of prayers to the divine. Below is a set of chants dedicated to the four elements and the cross-quarter ways.

<u>East</u>
The east corresponds with fire, dawn, the power and potency of the sun, sensuality, warding, protection, banishments, and defense. For spells that align with this subject of desire, one may use this chant below.

Fire in the east
I evoke your power
Hear my call
Aid me this hour

South

The south corresponds with earth, bodily healing, travel, prosperity, fertility, abundance, stability, hearth, and home. For spells that align with this subject of desire, one may use the following chant below.

West

The west corresponds with water, fluidity, intuition, dreams, emotions, mentality, and transitions. For spells that align with this subject of desire, one may use the following chant below.

North

The north corresponds with air, wind, weather, spirits, communication (with the living or those of the spirit world) necromancy, cursing, binding, and divination. For spells that align with this subject of desire, one may use the following chant below.

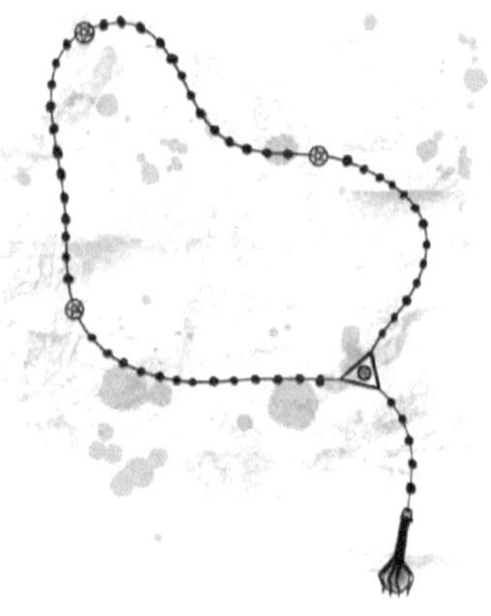

A simple way of casting a spell by chanting the beads might involve writing your desire as a present tense statement on a slip of paper (e.g. "Money comes to me easily"). Decide which way of the cardinal directions it corresponds with most and burn in a hearth or cauldron. As the written desire burns, face your chosen direction, and chant the full set of beads (one four-line chant per bead) while envisioning your spell manifesting into your life. You'll find at first you'll need to read the chant from the page, but as you repeat the words they will start to become a rhythm and by the time you get to the end, the chant will be flowing out of you imprinted deep in your psyche.

Chanting to the Old Ones

Items needed:
-A slip of paper and pen
-A white candle
-Water (optional: full moon water)
-A cauldron or fire-safe bowl
-Your beads

· This chant is designed to call upon the Old Ones as seen in the Preface; Absence, Existence, Desire, and Physicality. These beings are energetic forces older than time as we know it. They are the push for more and the outcome of achieving it. This chant is similar to the Petition to Invoking the Witches Devil and Witch Queen, but less traditional craft based. It involves spending time devoting your energies to evoke the Old Ones as if they were deified beings or archetypal figures and can be done within almost any religion or set of beliefs.

Light a candle and put forth an offering of water and incense. The incense should be sacred scents of Frankincense and Myrrh, Copal, or Dragon's Blood. Create your own sacred incense if desired. Draw out the magic square representing the old ones Absence, Existence, Desire, and Physicality. In the center of the magic square, write

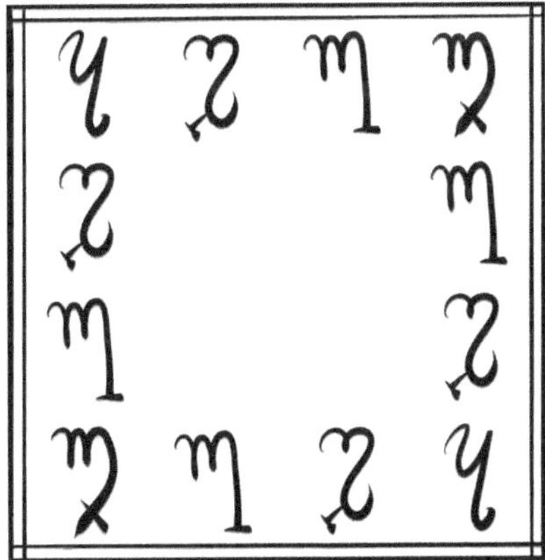

your reasonable desire clearly, consecrate it by bathing it in the smoke of the incense, and light the paper on fire with the candle. As it burns in a cauldron or fire-safe bowl, chant the beads with the following words.

From the void we came
Existence sprung
Desire for more
My will become

Chant the entirety of the beads 3 times round letting the words run together. As your mind drifts into a meditative state, pay close attention to what comes to you. Are you receiving thoughts, ideas, or images? Are there smells, tastes, or sounds that your senses pick up? This is a time of not only energy building but for communication with the wild spirit forces of the universe. This is an opportunity to begin building personal gnosis and spirit-led practices. You may want to make chanting and trance work a regular part of your craft.

While this rite is simple, it involves devotion to stilling the mind and connecting to the spirit world. It's not about the words of the chant. It's about the witch sending out a beacon of conjuration to the energies of Desire and Physicality to commune, to acknowledge the void and your existence in relation to it. It's a time to share a mental place and affect reality.

Scatter the ashes to the wind and give the water back to the earth the following sunrise.

Author's note: This spell is one of my personal favorites because it is accessible to practitioners at any level and as simple as it is, shows a level of commitment to your craft. To create a set of beads and devote time to chant on them to manifest your desires, is a way of taking your own personal altar with you anywhere you go to work magic. It also allows the witch to make their written petition extremely specific and detailed to be clear about what they hope to achieve. This is why I prefer to use present-tense statements. It sets my spell up to enact my desire within my reality as if it is already happening versus being in a perpetual state of waiting for it to happen. Being direct and specific in spell craft is important. Otherwise, you might end up with exactly what you asked for, but not how you expected to receive it. Be sure to document any spirit communications that come to you and outcomes from your rites.

Traditional witchcraft as a land-based practice has deeply informed my work. For that reason, the elements, as shown above, line up with the cardinal directions in a way that's somewhat more physical. The element of Air corresponds to the north as it's upwards. The element of Fire corresponds with the east to represent the rising sun. The element of Earth corresponds with the South as it's under our feet, and the element of Water corresponds to the West as there lies the Pacific Ocean. It's important to consider if this framework fits your practice. If not, feel free to use the information in this chapter and apply it you your set of beliefs as you see fit.

Gran's Grimoire

An Offering to the Fair folk

When making good with the fair folk of your land, offer a
bowl of milk and whisky outside in a place to be left to
them and say:

Fair folk of the wood • I offer spirits and milk
Keep me kindly in your eye • For I give reverence To your ilk

An Offering to the Birds

With a wand or your finger, draw a pentacle over a bowl of
bird feed and say the following to make good with the
messengers of aerial spirits.

The birds may come, the birds may go, they're always welcome here.
This bird feed I do bless for the birds far and near.

An Oaken Wand or Staff

Use a wand to channel energy in workings. Cut or gather a fallen branch of oak suitable to your needs, debark, and sand smooth to your liking. You may also stain it or carve sigils of significance if desired. Under the full moon, anoint the wand/staff with cunning oil, blood from your right hand, and ash from your ritual hearth/altar incense. As you anoint say the incantation.

Wand of oak • Wood of my land
Carry my will • From thought to hand

Under the moon • Consecrated this night
Blessed and charged • By this sacred rite

By blood of body • And ash of light
This wand and I • Are bound on this night

Kiss the wand and hold it at your heart's center with both hands and after several heartbeats say:

And so it is.

Success Oil (4)

Items needed:
-2oz carrier oil
-6 drops Bergamot essential oil
-2 drops of Ginger essential oil
-2 drops of Peppermint essential oil
-2 drops of Cedar essential oil
-A sprinkle of basil
-A sprinkle of powdered cicada shell

Blend on a Thursday, chant into the bottle 4 times, and close tight. Let sit in altar or hearth overnight and anoint your wrists before embarking on endeavors one would desire success in, especially financial and business.

By Monarda Fistulosa
And Spirits of success
A boon of good fortune
Upon this oil I do bless

Memory Oil (3)

Items needed:
-2oz carrier oil
-9 drops of Rosemary essential oil
-3 drops of Peppermint essential oil
-A few sprigs of Rosemary

Mix together on a Wednesday and chant into the bottle 8 times:

Peppermint sharp • Rosemary mind
Memory strong • Clear thoughts I find

Close and let sit overnight on your altar or hearth. Anoint temples to aid in memory preservation

A Tea for Prophetic Dreams (1)(2)

Herbs need:
-1Tsp of mugwort
-1Tsp of lemon grass

Simmer for 3-5 minutes, strain, and drink with honey before bed. As stirring say 3 times:

Prophecy come • Divine by dream
Show what's to be • To know the unseen

Do not consume if pregnant or trying to get pregnant.

A Pillow for Prophetic Dreams (1)

Sew a pillow or place a charm bag with three or more of these herbs in your pillowcase.

-marigold/calendula
-mugwort
-lemongrass
-vervain
-star anise

Use the same spoken charm as above under Prophetic Tea. Speak the charm 3 times into the bag before closing or into the pillow before sewing shut.

A Garlic Garland(1)

To protect your home from evil spirits or ill wishes, hang a garland of garlic by your entryways blessed by this charm.

This spirited home
This witches dwelling
This garland does guard
The garlic expelling

All spirits seeking my home
Who carry bane within
Cross my threshold they shall not
And keep all safe therein

To Bring Storms

Items needed:
-Paper and pen
-A large bowl
-Dirt from your land
-Water (full moon water would work well here)

Draw this sigil on paper and place atop a bowl of dirt from your land. Very slowly trickle the water over the paper till it's soaked while speaking the words below aloud.

The rain does come
From the sky
Water droplets
From way up high
Storm do come
Without delay
Clear blue skies
Go away

When the rain comes,
catch and bottle some of the water to save for the next time to call the rains again.

Author's note: This sigil is based on the alchemical symbols of water and air and several archetypal words associated with storms.

To Make Binary Divination Bones

Boil clean three chicken leg bones and anoint them with oil
of Artemisia (mugwort or substitute with wormwood). As
you rub the oil into the bones, chant the following charm 3
times, once for each bone.

Bones of my land
Only truth do tell me
If ye fall vertical
A yes my answer be
If the answer be no
On the horizon do fall
Spirits of my land
Your foresight I do call

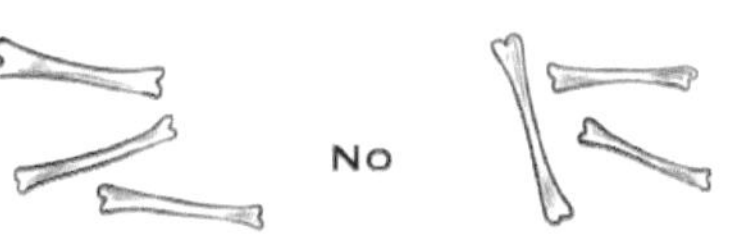

Once anointed the spirit of
artemisia has taken
residence in the bones to
speak yes or no responses
with the instructions you have given it. Ask a question and
toss the bones. Should 2 or more fall vertically (up and
down) your answer is yes. Should 2 or more bones fall
horizontally (laying sideways) your answer is no. Should
your response be unclear, ask again later.

To Ease Grief (3)

To ease grief, carry Hyacinth or Marjoram in a small charm
bag with some lemon peel and a scroll stating:

Grief be gone. Sadness withdrawn
I invite joy with this charm I employ.

A Wash to Clear, Cleanse, and Bless (1)

1 part water, 1 part rubbing alcohol with a sprinkle of hyssop, and a few drops of pine essential oil (avoid the essential oil if there are pets in the house. Instead, soak pine needles in the rubbing alcohol for 2-4 weeks). Use for floor wash, surface cleaner, and cleansing tools. While using, chant the charm till completion:

The hissing hyssop clears the way
The pine settles in blessed to stay

Smoke Cleanse to Remove Dark Entities from your Home (4)

-1 part Angelica
-1 part Nettles
-1 part Frankincense/Copal

Grind together in a clockwise manner on a Saturday till coarse.

When smoke cleansing a space, open windows and doors to a clear way of exit to unwanted energy/entities. Wave the smoke in the air while chanting in a commanding tone:

By the Spirit of Angels
By the Leaf and Stalk that stings
By resin oh so Holy
I excise all malevolent beings!

A Spell to Break a Bad Habit (1)

Grind together catnip and dragon's blood resin and burn over a hot coal. Breathe in while you write the habit on paper. Burn the paper while chanting the charm 13 times inhaling the incense.

Habit I break
Addiction unmake
Make no mistake
I'll no longer partake

To Catch a Thief (1)(2)

Into a fire throw marigold/calendula flowers and speak the cunning words:

A thief be caught, a thief be known
Be found who dare to steal from me
Their name be learned, their face be shown
Nevermore a burglar shall they be

Charm to Attract Love (3)

Carry a sachet of at least two of these herbs or more:
-Red rose petals
-Coriander seeds
-Dill
-Marjoram

On a Friday, place into a small red charm bag and say into it 7 times:

Spirits of earth • *Love, lust, and mirth*
My will I install • *Be my siren call*

Then close tight and carry with you.

Pine Cone Fertility Charm (3)

Place a pine cone under your bed to increase fertility. Say the charm 3 times and aim to conceive in that bed:

Babe of pine • *Come into my home*
Bring unto me • *A Babe of my own*

A Blessing of Lemons and Pins (5)

On a Sunday at sunset take a large lemon and with 36
colored pins (but no black), prick the fruit, and with each
pin say the cunning proclamation.

Blessings by the majestic sun
Good fortune by the lady moon
Aradian charm do I charge
Gifts of advantage so opportune

To Break a Love Spell (4)

Bless Pistachios with the following charm and feed them
to the afflicted.

By Pistacia Vera
Love spell be cracked
Little green tree nut
Infatuation retract

Spell to Encourage Harmony and Peace (4)

Herbs needed:
-1 part Skullcap
-1 part Dandelion flower
-1 part Rose Petals

These may be used in a white charm bag to encourage harmony around you or for remote work, carve the name of your target in a white candle or place it over a picture of them. Anoint it with cunning oil or olive oil, and dress the candle with the above herbs. Say the charm 9 times while envisioning your words coming out of your mouth and encircling the candle binding peace and harmony to your target. For a charm bag, speak the charm 9 times into the bag and close tightly and carry with you.

Skull be capped
Lion be dandy
Rose be dethorned
Harmonious as can be

Gentle and kind
No discord or strife
Promote only amity
A most peaceful life

An Apple Healing (3)

Cut an apple in half horizontally to expose the star of seeds in the center. Rub the apple halves over the afflicted person's body and chant 5 times for each point of the star:

Into this fruit
Into the seeds
I coax this illness
My word it heeds

Bring the apple halves back together and bind them with red string or ribbon while chanting 5 times:

Illness bound
Fruit encased
As it rots,
Be healed post haste

Then bury at a far-off crossroads or wooded area and do not look back.

Charm for Cash Flow

Put basil leaves or bay leaves in your wallet on a Thursday
and chant the words below 4 times to always be sure
you're never short on money. (1)

Money comes
And money goes
The basil/laural stays
And cash flows

A Stir to Sooth

Use this chant when stirring food or
beverage to help ease the anxieties and
tension of the one who is to consume it.
While stirring clockwise, speak the charm
aloud and envision the words coming out of
your mouth like ribbons being stirred directly
into your food or beverage.

To the right • I stir the pot
Round and round • Untie the knot

Let out the breath • Hackles unclench
Soothe the soul • Unbind the entrenched

Anxieties be gone • Relief do know
Into this dish • Solace I sew

To Turn Away Unwanted Affection (4)

On a turnip, carve the unwanted admirer's name and on the back carve this symbol for Affection. (Inspired by ASL for "love/affection")

Boil the turnip in water with sea salt and black pepper. After about 30 minutes, when it's tender, take it out of the water and mash in some fashion (large mortar and pestle, a fork and bowl, etc.) As you mash, chant the proclamation till the once full turnip is pulverized.

I turnip I turn over
I turn out your affection for me

Bring to a cemetery or bury in a place it will rest in peace undisturbed.

Send Ill-Luck to a Transgressor (1)

At sunset or midnight, take parsley to a crossroads and offer it to the Man in Black, and whisper the charm while sprinkling the parsley.

I send ill fortune
I send ill wishes
I give (Name of target)
To the king of the witches

Spit towards the east, south, west, then north. Walk away and don't look back.

Truth Potion

Items needed:
-1Tsp of Slippery elm
-1Tsp Skullcap
-1Tsp Cloves
-1Tsp Nettles
-A splash of Full Moon water
-1 cup of Vodka (may use white vinegar if necessary)
-A medium glass jar to store
-A medium dropper dark glass bottle

Place all the dry items in the jar, fill it with a cup of vodka, and a small splash of Full Moon water. Let sit for at least one full moon cycle (about 4 weeks) and shake daily to extract the spirits of the allies within. After the extraction cycle is complete, triple strain and seal in the medium dark glass dropper bottle. Before closing, speak the cunning words into the container and seal tight.

Spirits of pure candor
And allies of honesty
I consecrate this essence
Only the truth will set you free

Use just a few drops in sympathetic magic or on your target to extract the truth from them in most matters. While all the ingredients are non-toxic, due to allergies and some views on consent, it is not advised to plant in consumables.

Hex Breaking Tonic

Feed the afflicted a tonic of deeply steeped Nettles and/or Angelica root in boiling water till a deep green and say the chant 9 times over it while stirring counterclockwise:

I untwist
I unbind
This curse
So entwined
Out of body
Out of mind
Malice begone
No more maligned

Witch Bottles:

Bottle to Return a Witches Curse or Hex

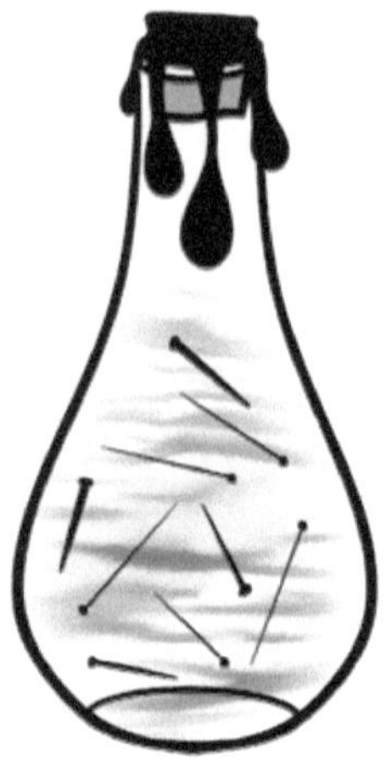

-Fill a glass bottle with:
-sharp pins/needles/iron nails
-urine of the afflicted person.

Place at the hearth by a blazing fire and wait for the urine to boil. The witch who cast the curse will begin to feel the pain of a full bladder forcing them to remove the curse. Should the bottle shatter in the heat, the witch who cast the curse will experience a complete rebound of their working back upon themselves.

If this method is not available to you, I suggest a black candle with nails and pins stuck into it. Have it affixed to the center of a small bowl and fill it less than halfway up with the afflicted's urine. The witch who hexed/cursed you will have till the candle self-extinguishes in the urine to reverse the magic or it will return to fall back on them. See The Black Book for a third alternative.

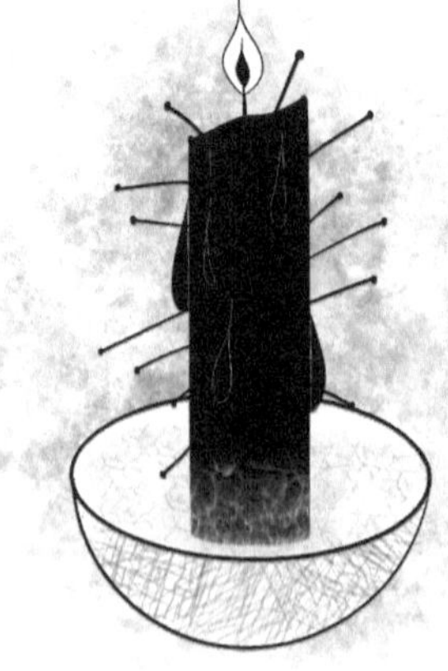

A Protective Bottle for Future Malevolence

Fill a glass bottle with:
-pins / needles
-iron nails
-broken glass / mirror.
May every household
member place:
-fingernail & toenail
clippings
-hair
-urine

Seal with a cork and wax to never again be opened. Bury on your land near your place of dwelling and all future malevolent curses, hexes, and workings will be trapped by your decoy bottle instead of making their way to you.

Author's note: Should burying not be an option, a potted plant is fine or placed in the back of a spare cabinet somewhere it will be forgotten.

Devil's Domination Rattle

Items needed:
-A taglock of your target (hair/nails, personal item, picture, handwriting/signature, or paper with their name and birthday as a last resort)
-an opaque jar or small non-translucent box
-one fully dried datura seedpod

Hold the taglock over the vessel and speak aloud 3 times:

(Name) I invite you into this vessel
Make yourself at home
Accept my hospitality
I offer you a throne

This aspect of this sympathetic hex lulls your target into a false sense of security. Place the taglock inside to get settled in. Then hold the dried datura seedpod over it, spit on it, and say aloud 3 times:

Damned Devils Berries
Most manipulative thorn apple
Under my chokehold I place you
With this devil's domination rattle

Place the dried Datura seedpod in the small opaque jar/box, close, and shake it like a rattle. Once it has pricked its way into the psyche of your target, you may write commands, ideas, or thoughts you'd like to plant into their mind. Then shake it up to activate after each slip of paper is added to the vessel.

An Apotropaic Horseshoe

As an alternative to garlic, keep an old horseshoe by the entryways of your home so all malefic magic sent one's way gets turned right back out. Anoint it in cunning oil, breath on it deeply on it 3 times and say the charm 3 times.

By iron and rust, no malevolence shall pass!

To Banish Nightmares

Place a charm bag of mullein and/or vervain and a crossroads nail collected at sunset under your pillow to protect you from nightmares. Before closing speak into the bag or write in a small scroll the following statement. (1)(2)

My dreams are guarded
Nightmare's be gone
My sleep is sacred
From dusk to dawn

The Red Book

The Three Knots of the Red Mother

This spell will allow you to create an all-purpose knot charm to transform yourself. This can be used for healthy motivation, glamor, improve a skill, adjust bad habits, and generally bring about change in your life. Under a full moon, write your reasonable desire on paper, give it 3 breaths of life, and burn it and set aside the ashes for later. Cut 9 strands of red embroidery thread the length best to fit your wrist. Tie the first knot to bind the threads together at the end and say:

*By knot of one
this spell's begun*

Then break the 9 strands into 3 sets of 3 and begin to braid. As you do, focus on your desire and chant:

*By mother in red
My words twist and bind
My desire most true
I weave fate's design*

When it's to the end, tie it off and say:

By knot of two
This spell be true

Then spit into the ashes and create a black paste. Apply it to the braid and rub it into the crevices. Tie it around your dominant wrist and say:

As it is written
By knot of three
As I will it
So shall it be

Your desire shall manifest in your life and push you to take steps toward your goal or transformation. To remove the bracelet would break the spell and sometimes that's a good thing.

Protection Braid

Braid a three-strand braid with red embroidery thread and a few strands of your hair while chanting:

The mother in red
Plucked a hair from my head
Bound it in thread
While these words be said
Protect me!
Protect me!
Protect me!

*if hair is not an option, might I suggest soaking a simple braid in the Elixir of Protection seen in part II chapter 2.

Love thy Self

Bring to a rolling boil pink rose petals and spit in it the pot 3 times. Soak red embroidery thread in the potion and once cooled, chant while braiding:

The woman cloaked in crimson
Conjured a potion of rose
To weave in thread
Of deep scarlet red
Love for oneself be composed

Tie on your dominant wrist or ankle and wear for as long as necessary.

Red Fire

Items needed:
-A 4-6oz dark glass dropper bottle
-90%+ Isopropyl Alcohol
-1Tsp powdered Madder Root or Dragons Blood resin

Mix the crimson pigment with the alcohol in a glass for 30 minutes, triple strain, and store in the glass dropper bottle. Before closing speak the cunning words into the opening, seal, and shake well.

Flammable spirit
Red Mother evoked
Liquid so Crimson
Magic be stoked

This magical red liquid is a highly flammable elixir charged by the spirit of the Red Mother to be used in ritual flame. It can be used in spells to burn petitions in a cauldron, a hearth, or sprinkle on a campfire to prepare for magical rites. One way to use this is to drip a few teaspoons into a cauldron or fire-safe bowl, add sea salt to create a slushy stable burning medium, mix well with your wand or tool of choice, and light aflame. Use this quick burning fire to burn herbs, sigils, or petitions, while chanting or performing incantations.

An Amulet of Power and Potency

Items needed:
-A red charm bag or cloth to
make one
-The magic square of the Old
Ones with a fingerprint stamped
in a drop of blood from your left
pointer finger
-Earth from a crossroads
-River quartz from the liminal
space
where land meets water
-A found feather of your land
-13 Datura seeds or 3 dried Belladonna Berries (If
available. If not, consider mugwort or wormwood)
-Ritual ash from your hearth, altar, or workspace

This amulet is a spirit house of magical items carrying with
it the virtues of liminality. Gather the items and place them
into the bag or cloth and bind together. Before it is bound
or closed, whisper into the bag 3 times the following words
and carry it with you for added power and potency.

Spirits awaken of land and sky
Spirits I house of in between
Lend me your power, your cunning eye
Aid me as a traffic with the unseen

36 Knots of Healing

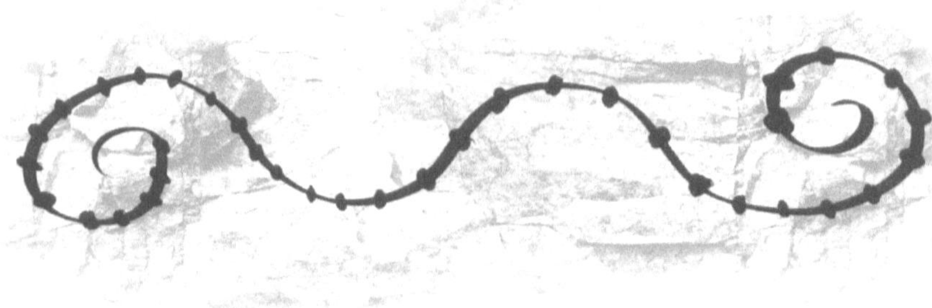

On a Sunday, take a thin red ribbon or some red
embroidery thread and tie 36 knots in it. With each knot,
say the following cunning words:

The Red Mother spins
The master thread bearer
She ties up the knots
That heal the ill wearer
May it bind all ailments
May it diminish disease
The Red Mother wills it
All maladies ease

Tie it around the ailing person's left wrist or ankle and
leave till healed.

A Mercurial Road Opener

On a Wednesday, burn Dandelions and draw out the Seal of Mercury. Stamp it with the blood of your dominant pinky finger, hold it between your palms at your heart's center, and say the cunning command 8 times.

Mercury, Old One, Divine Androgyne
Open all roads
Open all doors
Open all pathways of communication
May all signs be clear
May all paths to
Advantage and abundance
Be unblocked
By your seal
By your name
I evoke your power

Burn the seal and the spell has been cast. Be aware, opening roads to new opportunities inevitably will result in leaving behind things that no longer serve you.

An Amulet for Safe Travels

Items needed:
-A red charm bag or cloth to make one
-2 bones of a chicken wing (or crossroads nails)
bound into a cross with red thread
-Witches black salt
-A slip of paper with the following phrase written on it:

Just as the Red Mother crosses the land, sea, and sky, so shall the carrier of this amulet travel safely till they return home.

Roll up the slip of paper into a scroll and place all the items into the bag or cloth. Close, bind, or sew the bag shut and carry with you or gift to a dear one for safe travels.

A Charm of Defense

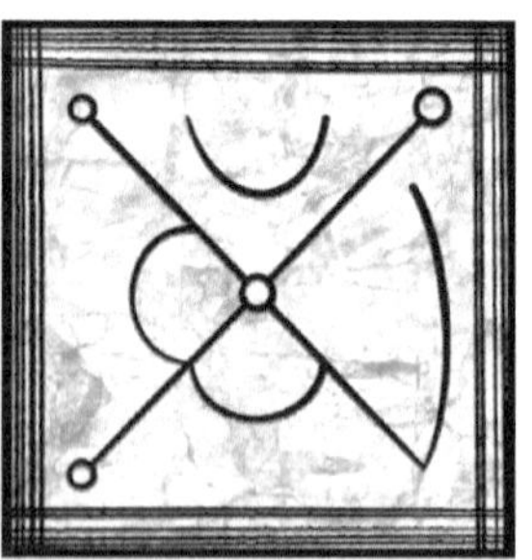

For a charm of defense in battle or conflict, on a Tuesday, draw the seal of Mars on paper and add to a red charm bag with 5 snake vertebrae and a rusty crossroads nail. On the back of the drawn seal, write the following phrase, close, and carry with you or gift to one in need of magical defense.

By the serpent of the crossroads and great sphere of red, defend whosoever carries this charm.

Self Confidence Charm (1)

In a cloth of red add yarrow, Thyme, Basil, dried poke berries (if available,) and rose quartz for self confidence and courage. Add one chicken wing bone or a found feather to lift your spirits. Add these items to the cloth and sew shut while chanting:

The red mother gave me her hand
She lifted me up from the land
A charm bag she sewed
Self confidence flowed
The flames of courage were fanned

Carry with you in moments of need.

Beads of Protection from Dark
Spirits of the Winter (1)

String a small garland of holly berries on red thread and hang by all entryways. For each berry chant the words:

Holly berry holly berry
Ripe, round, and red
In comes the cold
And the night takes hold
Evil spirits can't cross this thread

A Wash to Break a Hex (1)

Boil fresh juniper berries and green sprigs in a large pot for
20 min. Stir regularly and chant while stirring the charm 13
times. Use to wash objects or self.

Juniper evergreen
Hexes that may be unseen
Untwist unwind
Don't resist unbind
The mountain yew that washes clean

Divination Incense (4)

-1 part Mugwort
-1 part Dragons Blood
-1 part Wormwood
-1 part Star Anise

Grind in a mortar and pestle together clockwise chanting
the below charm till just coarse. Burn over a coal when
using divination tools to lift the veil between worlds.

Spirits of earth
And the divine
Bring second sight
Open my mind

To Wish Upon a Bay Leaf (4)

Write a reasonable wish upon a dry Bay Leaf and burn safely while chanting till ash.

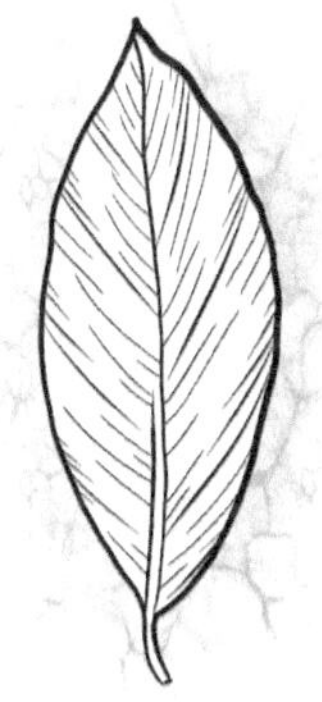

Spirit of Laurel
Leaf of Bay
Spark and sizzle
As I say
Such cunning words
My wish do grant
By Laurus Nobilis
This charm enchant

Scarlet Ink

Items needed:
-2oz of vodka
-2 Tbsp of Dragons blood (crushed)
-2 Tbsp of macerated Poke Berries (if available)
-Gum Arabic powder
-Double boiler
-Small jar to store

On a full moon, warm over a double boiler and let simmer to extract the scarlet nature of the resin and macerated berries for 15-30 min. Remove what's left of the resin and berries and add Gum Arabic little by little till the consistency of blood. As you stir, chant the following 13 times:

Bottle and leave on your altar or workspace overnight. Use in petitions, sigils magic, and any magical writing. You may substitute the vodka for vinegar if necessary but might need longer cooking.

To Repel Negativity

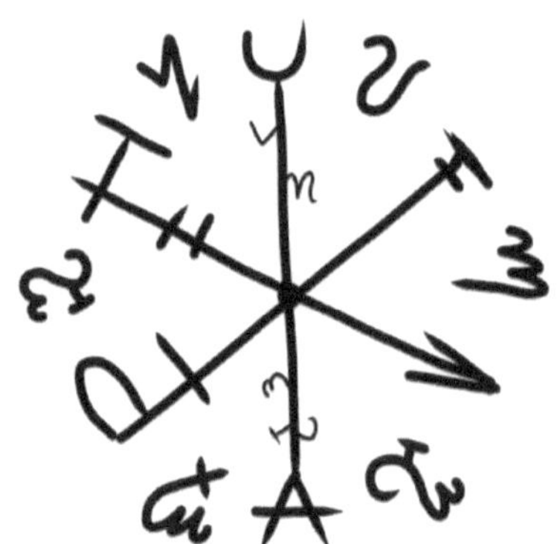

Draw the sigil on paper and spit on it 3 times to charge then carry with you, brew coffee or tea over it, put it under your seat in your vehicle, or gift to a loved one to protect them from negative energy.

The Green Book

A Healing Candle for Our Mother in Green

-Herbs to use:
-Lemon balm
-Fever few
-Mugwort
-Sage
-Yarrow
-Shepards purse

Carve the name of the person in need of healing on a green or white candle, anoint it in Cunning Oil (olive oil will do if necessary,) and dress it with these healing herbs. Alternative: write the affliction on a picture of the target and place a candle on top of it. Then you can encircle the candle and picture with these herbs. (I suggest picking 3 or more of the healing herbs from the options listed based on availability to you) Light the candle and call to the Green Mother as a symbol, and energy source for healing.

Lady viridian • Veiled in chartreuse
Lend me your aid • All ailments reduce.
By spirits of earth • May you intervene.
Affliction begone • Dear Mother in green

Say repeatedly till you build up a rhythm of trance and you feel the mother has heard your petition and let the candle burn out naturally.

To Calm the Nerves and Center Oneself

Carry a charm bag of Rosemary, Lavender, and a small
scroll with the statement written upon it:

Centering Mary and Lady Lavandula
From the Green Mothers garden
Calm me now

In moments of distress, breath in the aroma deeply for 10
breaths. Close your eyes. Calm the heart and the mind.

A Charm for a Sunburn

Rub fresh-cut Aloe Vera jelly or a pre-made aloe gel onto a
sunburn and say the charm 3 times.

The sun was angry and spat fire down
Mother of the woods came in her green gown
With her balm of aloe
She took all the pain
She calmed the heat
The fire now slain

An Anti-inflammatory

-A tea of Oregano can be used as a general anti-
inflammatory, and the oil of oregano can be used as a
topical anti-inflammatory and anti-bacterial. A salve with
oregano essential oil is a long used antimicrobial for topical
surface wounds. (10)

A Healing Amulet

Items needed:
-A green or white charm bag or cloth to make one
-A pinch of Yarrow
-A pinch of Mugwort
-A pinch of Shepherds Purse
-A pinch of Feverfew
-A pinch of Lemon Balm
-An Abracadabra triangle

```
A B R A C A D A B R A
A B R A C A D A B R
A B R A C A D A B
A B R A C A D A
A B R A C A D
A B R A C A
A B R A C
A B R A
A B R
A B
A
```

This amulet is made to be a spirit house for the healing herbs from the Green Mother's garden. It uses the ancient descending Abracadabra triangle alongside the herbs to heal you or a dear one. Place at least three of the herbs listed and the triangle drawn on paper into the bag or cloth and before closing, binding, or sewing it shut, speak the cunning words into the bag 3 times. The ailing person should then wear it at all times till they are well.

"Abracadabra," said the Green Mother
Into the ear of the sick
"I've gathered herbs from my garden
And come to heal you up quick"
The magic word took away
All ailments from the afflicted
A gift from the Green Mother
No more shall they be constricted

A Tea for Fever and Headache (1)

-1Tsp. Peppermint
-1Tsp. Feverfew
Steep in boiled water for 3 minutes and strain. Sweeten as desired and as you stir, chant the charm 3 times. (May also substitute Lemon Balm or Thyme)

The mother in green came from the woods
She brought with her herbs of health
She brewed a potion to cure the sick
Then slipped back into the night with stealth

A Poultice to Stop blood (1)

Macerate yarrow and clean water to create a thick mixture to pack on a freshly cleaned wound to stop the blood. Place your dominant hand over it and move your hand in a clockwise circle and say 3 times:

The Lady in Green jumped off the ledge
She stumped them all at the cliff's edge
Just like this yarrow stops the blood
These veins shall heal and no more flood

A Tea to Sleep Deeply (1)

--1Tsp Valerian root
-1Tsp Chamomile
-1Tsp Lavender
Bring 3 cups of water to a rolling boil. Add the lavender
and valerian root in and boil for 20 minutes. Strain and
steep the chamomile for 3-5 minutes. Strain and sweeten as
desired. Stir while saying the following charm and drink
before bed.

I dream of a sleep so deep
Nothing shall disturb my slumber
I dream of a sleep so deep
Nothing shall disturb my slumber

A Tea for a Sore Throat (1)(6)

-2Tsp Common sage
-1Tsp Peppermint
Steep in a cup of boiled water for 15 min. Strain and
sweeten as desired. Stir and chant 3 times then drink. (May
substitute for thyme)

Little frog little frog
From tongue to throat do slide
Take the pain
De-inflame
Then dissolve down deep inside

Author's note: This charm is built off the healing power of common sage. Its Latin name Salvia derived from salvo means "to save" or "heal". It is believed that folk names were given to many of these herbs and plants, and some have suggested that "frog" or "toad" was the folk representation of Sage. While these code names for many practical herbs did exist, there's not enough evidence to show that it was as popular and deceptive as Shakespeare's witches in Macbeth. The concept for this spell comes from two sources, Wortcunning and The Devil's Plantation by Nigel G Pearson. The first tells the history of using teas and tonics of sage for colds and sore throats. The second source cites an old cold healing charm from the 19th century that suggests a medicine of three frogs powered lungs consumed, followed by a charm that tells the frogs within to heal the afflicted person of all maladies. Were they using real frog lungs or three common sage leaves? Who can say?

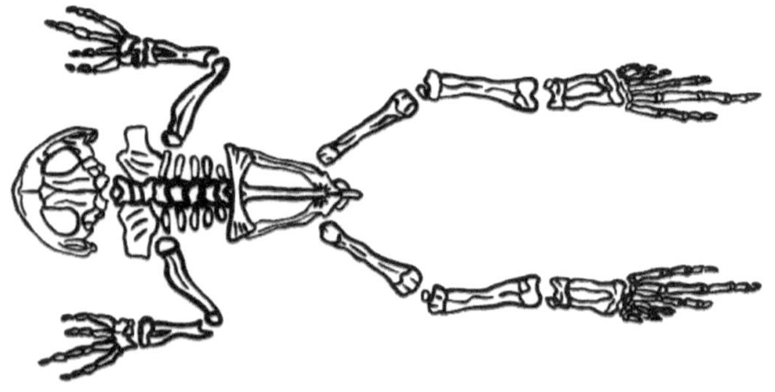

Garlic to Heal and Harm (1)

Rub a clove of garlic over an ailment of the body in a counterclockwise direction and say three times:

The green mother went out to pick
From the meadow of wild garlic
The cloves held secrets
Within their uniqueness
They heal and remove ailments quick

Dispose of the clove or bury it at a crossroads to banish the ailment
-OR-
Cook into a meal to feed to another to transfer the ailment to them.

A Charm Bag for Melancholy (10)

Carry St, John's Wart in a small charm bag or sachet to combat mild depression and melancholy. It always blooms around the summer solstice so it carries with it a sunny virtue. Into the Charm bag, chant the following 9 times.

Flowers that bloom
At the sun's utmost height
Bring a brighter disposition
And rose-colored sight

For Maladies of the Heart

Items needed:

-1Tsp Mothers Heart/shepherd's purse heart-shaped seed pods

-1Tsp Foxglove flowers

-1Tsp Turmeric

-A red or white charm bag

Fill the charm bag with each herbal ally and before closing, speak into the bag the incantation 3 times. Place it under the mattress of the afflicted person.

Oh yellow spice and bright fairy cap
Steady the beating heart
The blood pumps blue from head to toe
From this vital organ illness depart
The peppergrass does enliven the veins
And together they form a triad
Benefic and poison tempered by spice
Bring their heart health back ironclad

For Remote Healing of the Heart

Grind the three herbs listed above into a medium-grain powder. Anoint a red or white candle in cunning oil or olive oil, dress the candle with the herbs, and place it over a picture of the afflicted person or atop a taglock of them. Burn while chanting the incantation 9 times.

Option 2: Make a poppet of the afflicted person with the herbs listed above and chant the incantation over the doll 9 times.

For Insect Stings

Grind fresh basil leaves with a few drops of water (full moon water if available) to create a poultice for insect stings. Apply to the sting and chant in groups of three the charm below. (10)

Take the sting. Take the sting. Take the sting.

For Troubled Sleep

-Rub Lavender oil on your temples and neck while chanting the charm below for trouble sleeping. (10)

Waking world be gone
Slumber come deeply
Oh soothing spirit
Lavendula bespell me

General Curatives

-Always keep Rosemary growing in your garden. Gather it at sunrise in bundles to have about the home to protect the dwellers from evil spirits and ill wishes. (2)

-Grow Holly near your home and wear a charm of Holly to keep safe from lightning. (2)

-Brew Dandelion leaf tea as a dietetic and to treat gastrointestinal discomfort. (10)

-Drink a Dill or Basil tea brewed lightly for gas and flatulence. (10)

-A hot bath with Mustard seeds will ease aches and pains of the body and joints, as well as reduce stress and tension in the body. (10)

-Toss Shepherds Purse in a fire and say the name of one afflicted with illness to send them healing well wishes.

-Sprinkle dried Wormwood in clothing storage to combat moths. (10)

-Use fresh or dried muddled Chamomile to reduce the pain of a toothache. Apply it directly to the afflicted area. (1)

-Chew Licorice Root before kissing a romantic partner to increase their affections for you (1)

The Black Book

A Call for Our Mother in Black

For a punishment that fits the crime, carve the name and birthdate of your transgressor onto a black candle or set a black candle atop a picture of them. Set it in your window to be seen by the shadows of the night and light it then chant the evocation below 13 times.

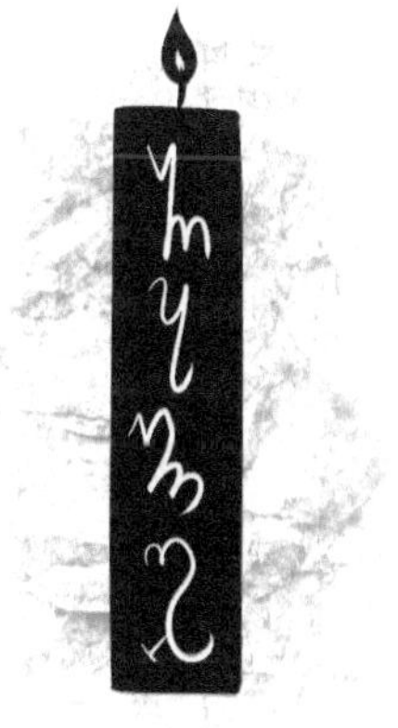

Mother in Black I call your name
Hear my plea through shadow by flame
To punish the wicked your name I enlist
Aid me now in this curse I twist

Nettle to Calm its own Sting

Muddle fresh nettle leaves or a few dried nettle leaves and a few drops of water then rub onto the afflicted area and chant 3 times.

The leaves will soothe the stalk that stings.
The burn within shall no more cling
Blessing and bane grow on the same stalk
Gates that open can also block
What can harm can also heal
Nettle sting conceal unfeel

Curse of the Seeds that Wither

Items needed:
-13 Datura seeds
-Soil
-A garden or planter pot
-A taglock of your target (hair, nails, signature or handwriting, a small personal item, picture, or their name and birthdate written 3 times on paper.
-Dark Moon Water

This spell will wither away the strength, health, and general well-being of your target. At sunset or midnight, fill the planter pot 2/3 the way up and place the target's taglock there. Lay the Datura seeds atop the taglock and sprinkle a bit of Dark Moon Water over it. Say the following cursed words and cover with the rest of the soil.

Our Mother in Black pricked her finger
And drew a drop of blood
She poisoned those who crossed her
With this most baneful bud
Devil's trumpet roots did sprout
Green stalks began to grow
And withered away all that was
Of the one who crossed her below.

Water every other day and nurture it to grow. As it does, your target will receive the effects. If your plant fails to thrive or dies the curse will falter and die as well. This can be due to lack of care, the targets personal protections warding the curse, or them taking steps to remove it.

Authors note: Should Datura not thrive where you live or be available to you, consider another baneful or poisonous herb that agrees with your climate. More European or northern dwellers may benefit more from Belladonna or Nightshade. In the south, Pokeweed might be another advantageous option. If this is the case, change the word "Devil's trumpet" in the incantation to "Nightshade", "Pokeweed", etc to amend the verbiage.

To Inflict Untold Malefic Intent Upon a Trespasser

-13 Porcupine needles or traditional pins
-A purple onion
-A picture or taglock of your target

Cut the onion in half and place the taglock or picture of your target in the center of the two halves. Use the needles to fasten the two haves back together, locking your target inside the sharp overpowering onion. With each pin, say this charm a total of 13 times.

Mother in black
Flew down from the sky
She poisoned the wicked
Leaving no trace behind

Then take it to a cemetery and bury it in the most northern corner. **Warning:** This curse as written is not specific and can result in a plethora of sinistral outcomes. Keep that in mind. If you'd like to be more specific, write out your detailed malefic intent on the picture before placing it in the onion.

To Compel and Control (7)

You'll need:
-Grains of Paradise (Guinea peppers)
-A picture of your target
-A mortar and pestle
-A black candle
Grind up the Grains of Paradise in a mortar and pestle counterclockwise. Place the grains atop the photo and light

the candle. Hold it above the photo and allow it to melt and drip onto the picture, the pooling black wax sealing the ground grains to your target. As it's dripping, chant the below enchantment 13 times.

From the swamp emerged the Mother in black
Paradise peppercorns did the lady crack
The grains consumed attach to the soul
She fed them to those she wished to control
Once consumed does she compel
Those in the thralls of her dark spell

They will now be most malleable to your suggestion, and agreeable to your domination.

A simpler version of this spell is to say the enchantment 13 times while grinding the grains and then using it in food to be consumed only by the intended target if possible.

A Spoken Charm to give Someone the Day they Deserve

Stare directly at your target with all your might, spit ever so unnoticeably in their direction, and say under your breath with deep feeling:

The Lady in Red met the Lady in Black
Blessing and bane do they serve
Together they came to grant the one in my sight
The day which they most truly deserve

Return to Sender (1)

Items needed:
-1 part Nettles
-1 part Hyssop
-1 small purple onion

Put the onion chopped in quarters, the Nettles and/or Hyssop in a sheer sachet or generic muslin fabric bag, then from head to fingertips to toes, graze it across your body. Envision the Nettles clinging to the sticky hex peeling it off of you binding it to the Onion and, and neutralizing with the Hyssop. Chant the incantation below while rubbing the curse off your body 13 times

What you cast
I now send back
Thirteen times
Your own attack
Removed from me
Now cast your way
Thirteen times
Without delay

Immediately take to a cemetery, graveyard, or crossroads away from your home. Empty the contents of the sachet there, walk away without looking back, and throw the sachet away.

Banishing Powder

-1Tsp Cloves
-1Tsp Nettles
-1Tsp Black salt
-1Tsp Black pepper
-1Tsp Datura leaves (if available)

Grind together in a sinistral direction (counterclockwise) chanting the charm till a fine powder.

Spirited spice
Banishing nettle
Salt and ash
Grind and unsettle

Use this powder in banishing spells or workings. Toss into a fire with a taglock of your target. Coat a black candle in Cunning oil, dress it in the powder, and burn over a taglock/picture of your target. Blow directly on their home or doorstep if safe and possible. One might use this suggested chant to direct your spell.

Begone to the blackness
By herbs of bane
Banished from my life
Your presence shan't remain

Author's Note It is my sincere belief that there is no light without the dark. You cannot heal if you do not understand how to harm, and the cunning path of a witch is wise and crooked. Witchcraft is dangerous and a serious practitioner makes education and knowledge of both blessing and bane the forefront of their craft.

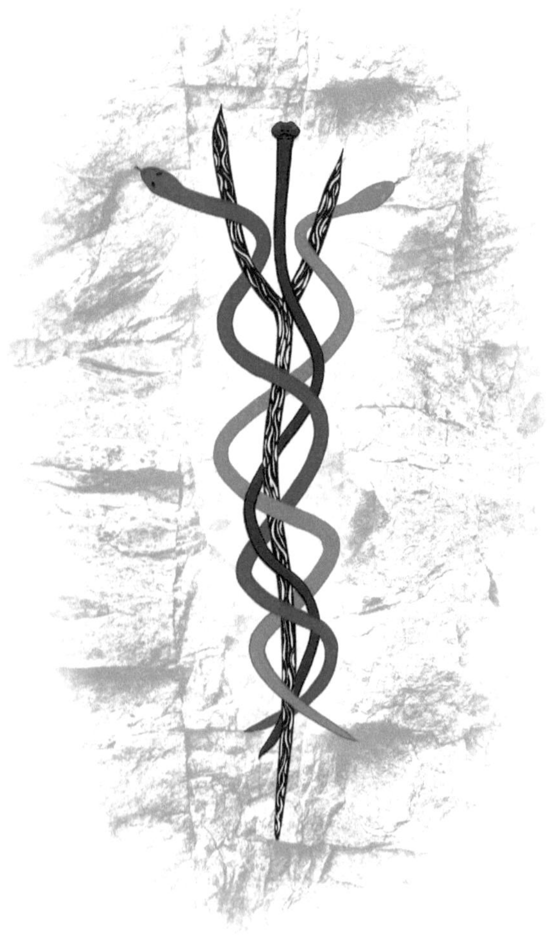

Three Wise Healers: a Revelation of the Sisters who Never Were

These entities are three nameless sisters who were birthed into a narrative that told a story of practical magic. They were inspired by a piece of art, unfurled into a tale, and grew into three spirit archetypes. These narrative-created beings are bodiless energies that represent three aspects of healing.

The first spirit is red and represents a connection to blood. This shade carries with it the inclination to heal wounds.

The second spirit is black and represents absence and removal. This shade carries with it the inclination to take away pain.

The third spirit is white and represents purity and new beginnings. This shade carries the inclination to purify the body and finalize the healing process inside and out.

In the tradition of the Graeae, the Graces, and the Gorgons, these healers are part of a triad, each with their own purpose but dependent upon each other. By knowing their story, and seeing oneself in the three nameless healers, a witch may step into their power and channel it through their craft.

How to use this Charm

This narrative charm may be used as a spoken chant over a fresh/healing wound or bodily ailment. Hold your dominant hand over the ailment and speak the charm above a whisper so the vocal cords at least vibrate minimally.

This charm may also be used for remote healing. Over a picture of your target with their name and birthday written upon it (if available,) place a red candle, a black candle, and a white candle encircled in mugwort, yarrow, and or lemon balm. Light the candles, envision your target at peak health, and chant the spoken charm three times. Let the candles burn out.

There once were three wise healers
One with hair as red as blood
One as black as a raven
And one as fair as flax
The first one healed your wounds
The second took your pain
And the third made you whole again

Rites of the Flaming Tree:
and other Charms of the Heart

To Attract a Romantic Partner

On a Friday (if possible), grind together pink dried Crepe Myrtle petals. Carve your full name and birthdate in a red or pink taper candle and charge your name with a drop of blood from your left ring finger. Anoint the candle with cunning oil (or olive oil) and roll in the dried Crepe Myrtle. Light the candle and chant the incantation 7 times.

My long lost lover • Come and find me
My sweet soulmate • Come to set me free
My companion for life • I long to know you
My partner my love • With a heart so true
I call out to the winds • To bring me true love
Make their way to me • By the heavens above
By all that is • And by all that will be
Bring my long lost love to me

To Attract a Lustful Lover

In cloth of red, gather red Crepe Myrtle flowers and close, bind up, or sew shut to create a sachet/charm bag while speaking the words of the story then carry with you.

Option 2: Write the words of the story on paper, roll or fold it up, and place it inside the bag with the red petals.

The tree stretched taller than ever before, its branches sticking straight out reaching for the melodic notes in the air. The crowd gathering watched in wonder as the fuchsia blooms deepened to a scarlet red as if its limbs were cut open bleeding soft plumes of ruffled petals.

The villagers could see the waves of heat now emanating from their sacred tree once so cool, pure, and white, the branches now erect, glistening like rubies in the moonlight. The singer came forward and the townspeople parted as they strode nearer singing their song.

The tree no longer able to be still started to quiver and the crimson flowers began to spark. The crowd stood back as flames burst from the tree, branches covered in small explosions of fire.

To Bring Two Lovers Together

Take two pink/red taper candles. Carve your name and birthdate in one candle and the targets on the other. (Extra: use a sharpened scribe created from Crepe Myrtle wood) anoint both in cunning oil or olive oil and bind together in red embroidery thread near the base. Sprinkle dried crushed pink Crepe Myrtle flowers all over the bound candles and stand upright on a fire-safe surface. Light the wicks and say the passage from the story below. Let the candles burn down together till melded. Do not let burn all the way down. Once burnt about halfway and thoroughly melted together, rap in red cloth and put somewhere to keep safe. If the spell relic is ever seen by your bound partner or the candles are ever separated, the spell will break.

They all watched and the singer was drawn forward unafraid of the burning tree. The flames died down and the singer approached the giant pile of ash. The smoke cleared and a gasp rang out. There in the pile of dying cinders stood a figure, a human figure. The magic of the song had ignited something deep with the sacred tree. Something its soul had never known… it's mate. The singer's song carried by the winds blew the ash away and they came together and embraced. "Your sweet melody has ignited a passion within me," said the figure. "What do I call you, my love?"
(Say their full name/names 3 times)

Lust Oil

You'll need:
-2oz carrier oil
-6 drops Rose Essential Oil
-5 drops Patchouli Essential Oil
-1 drop Ginger Essential Oil
-A sprinkle of red/fuchsia Crepe Myrtle blossoms

Blend together on a Friday and say the chant into the bottle 7 times then close tightly to sit on altar or hearth overnight. Wear very sparingly in erogenous zones (3)

Lust and sex
Blood to groin
Arousal Apex
Longing loins

Lust Wine (4)

Sprinkle a bit of Cardamom in a glass of warm red wine, encircle the glass with red/fuchsia Crepe Myrtle petals, and stir clockwise while chanting 7 times and drink:

Liquid lust
Spice and wine
By flaming tree
Libido unwind

To Freeze a Romantic Partner Out

On a Saturday, take a handful of Crepe Myrtle seed pod husks and a taglock of your target like hair, nails, or a small personal item. A picture or paper with their name and birthdate written on it 3 times will work if necessary. Mix the taglock and the seed pods in a small jar or container and add water. Stir counterclockwise and say the icy words 3 times.

Heart be frozen
Lover's eyes turn away
Your love for (me/ name)
Has gone bleak and grey
Into the ice
I cast your affection
Desire freeze
In this crepe myrtle suspension

Then put it in your freezer till ice.

Talismans of the Seven Holy Siblings

Should you find yourself with a desire or in need of magical intercession, a petition can be made into a talisman and enchanted by one of the Seven Holy Siblings. To create and enchant a talisman, reference the parable in part I, chapter 12 to decide which Sibling is best aligned with your desire: Sunday, Monday, Tuesday, Wednesday, Thursday, Friday, or Saturday. On that day, write out your desire on a slip of paper, and draw the planetary seal atop it. Then fold it up like a small pocket-size letter and chant the evocation over it as many times as directed based on planetary numbers. When done, seal it closed with wax and carry it with you. (8) (9)

Oh holy Sunday
I call upon your temple of the Sun
I evoke your power
Your virtue
Your celestial force
Fulfill my petition
Through shining light
Strength health and vitality
Oh happy star of good fortune
May the galaxy align
Under the might of the Sun
Imbue this talisman
With the spirit of my desire
Made real and true

Chant 9 times

Oh holy Monday
I call upon your temple of the Moon
I evoke your power
Your virtue
Your celestial force
Fulfill my petition
From Sky to sea
May the tides be pulled
Emotions stirred
And the veil be lifted
Under the might of the Moon
Imbue his talisman
With the spirit of my desire
Made real and true

tuesday tuesday tuesday tuesday

Oh holy Tuesday
I call upon your temple of Mars
I evoke your power
Your virtue
Your celestial force
Fulfill my petition
Great defender full of strength
Victorious in conflict
Virile and assertive warrior
Be my conquering arm
Under the might of Mars
Imbue this talisman
With the spirit of my desire
Made real and true

Wednesday Wednesday Wednesday

Seal of Mercury Seal of Mercury Seal of Mercury

Wednesday Wednesday Wednesday Wednesday

Seal of Mercury Seal of Mercury Seal of

Chant 8 times

Oh holy Wednesday
I call upon your temple of Mercury
I evoke your power
Your virtue
Your celestial force
Fulfill my petition
Keeper of memories
Road opener and discoverer
Great communicator and philosopher
Oh androgyne Spirit
Under the might of Mercury
Imbue this talisman
With the spirit of my desire
Made real and true

thursday thursday thursday

Oh Holy Thursday
I call upon your temple of Jupiter
I evoke your power
Your virtue
Your celestial force
Fulfill my petition
Oh gainful giant of abundance and success
A loyal leader most decorated and honored
So prosperous in hearth and home
Under the might of Jupiter
Imbue this talisman
With the spirit of my desire
Made real and true

friday friday friday friday

seal of venus seal of venus seal of venus

friday friday friday friday friday

seal of venus seal of venus seal of

Chant 7 times

Oh holy Friday
I call upon your temple of Venus
I evoke your power
Your virtue
Your celestial force
Fulfill my petition
Oh great lover of beauty and lust
Defender of romance and friendship
Fertile spirit of new creation
Under the might of Venus
Imbue this talisman
With the spirit of my desire
Made real and true

saturday saturday saturday

seal of saturn seal of saturn seal of saturn

seal of saturn seal of saturn seal of saturn seal of

saturday saturday saturday saturday saturday

Oh holy Saturday
I call upon your temple of Saturn
I evoke your power
Your virtue
Your celestial force
Fulfill my petition
Priest of physicality and wisdom
Being of land, death, and decay
By forces of chaos, limitation,
And twisted spirits of malice and manipulation
Under the might of Saturn
Imbue this talisman
With the spirit of my desire
Made real and true

Saturn talismans created to hex or curse are to be buried at a crossroads.

Authors note: You will see many spells with an adjoining number in part III of the Cunning Compendium. Everything in this book has been written by me but I have used several resources for historical information and herbal/planetary correspondence. They can be sourced back to the books below.

1. Wortcunning, Nigel G Pearson
2. The Black Toad, Gemma Gary
3. Magical Herbalism, Scott Cunningham
4. Encyclopedia of Magical Herbs, Scott Cunningham
5. Aradia Gospel of the Witches, Charles Leland
6. The Devil's Plantation, Nigel G Pearson
7. The Poison Path Herbal, Coby Michael
8. Traditional Witchcraft: a Book of Cornish Ways, Gemma Gary
9. The Three Books of Occult Philosophy, Henry Cornelius Agrippa
10. Culpeper's Complete Herbal, Nicholas Colpeper

Bibliography

Agrippa, Henry Cornelius. *The Three Books of Occult Philosophy*. Llewelyn Publications. 2018. Originally 1531

Colpeper, Nicholas. *Culpeper's Complete Herbal*. Union Square & Co. 2019. Originally 1653

Caroll, Peter. *Liber Null and Psychonaut*. Weiser books. 1987

Cunningham, Scott. *Encyclopedia of Magical Herbs*. Llewelyn Publications. 1985

Cunningham, Scott. *Magical Herbalism*. Llewelyn Publications. 1986

Gary, Gemma. *The Black Toad*. Troy Books. 2016

Gary, Gemma. *Traditional Witchcraft: a Cornish Book of Ways*. Troy Books. 2008

Gary, Gemma. *The Devil's Dozen*. Troy Books. 2015

Harner, Michael J. *Hallucinogens and Shamanism*. O for University Press. 1973

Hine. Phil. *Condensed Chaos*. New Falcon Publications. 1995

Kelden. *The Crooked Path*. Llewelyn Publishing. 2020

Kelden. *The Witches Sabbath*. Llewelyn Publishing. 2022

Leland, Charles Godfrey. *Aradia the Gospel of the Witches*. David Nutt. *1899*

Michael, Coby. *The Poison Path Herbal*. Park Street Press. 2021

Morgan, Lee. *A Deed Without a Name*. Moon Books. 2013

Pearson, Nigel G. *The Devils Plantation*. Troy Books. 2016

Pearson, Nigel G. *Treading the Mill*. Troy Books. 2017

Pearson, Nigel G. *Wortcunning*. Troy Books. 2019

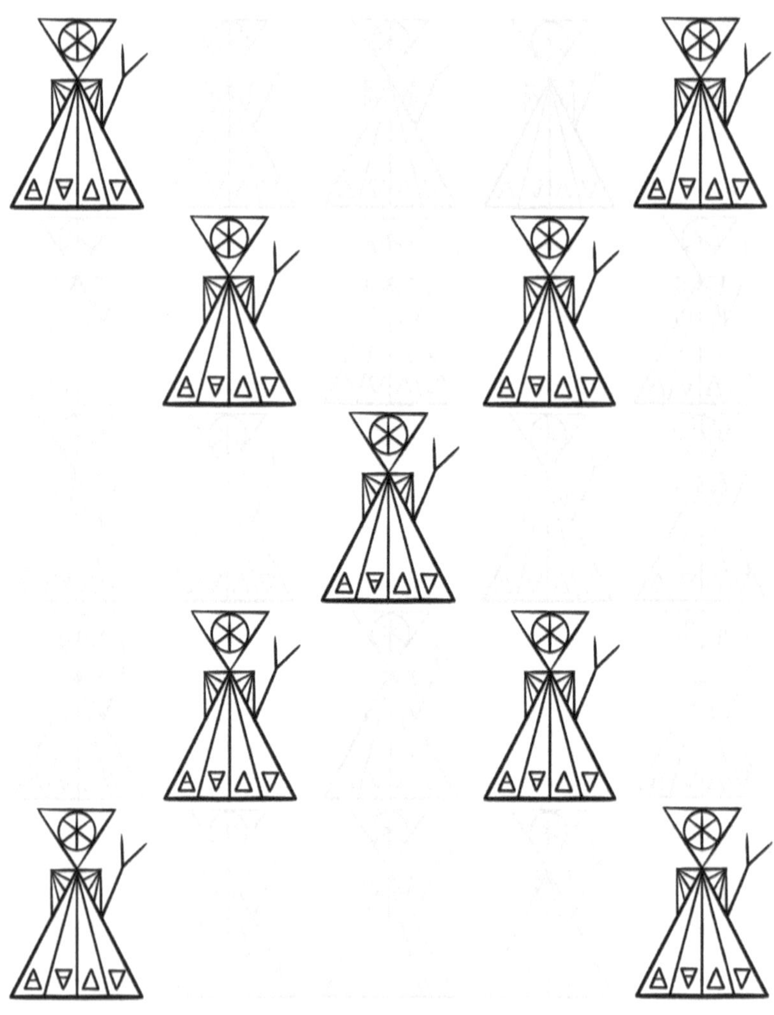

Author's final note: By now you may have noticed that not everything from all of the stories and poems is explicitly spoon-fed to the reader down to every detail. Some of the magic seen in Parts I and II are not elaborated on in Part III. Many of the characters don't even have names. This book is an inspiration with many very clear lessons in the magical arts but written for the cunning. Put yourself in the character's place. Be one with the stories within these pages. Take care to read between the lines, and if some instructions seem vague, it's because they are supposed to be. Adapt these tales and figures to your region; your climate; your life; your magic; your craft. Always be seeking new ideas and magics to learn. Be imaginative. Be creative. Be receptive. And most important of all, be cunning.

Marshall the Witch of Southern Light

Be
Cunning